Dual Relationships in Counselling & Psychotherapy

Ethics in Practice Series

Ethics in Practice edited by Tim Bond is a series of short, practical guides to ethical issues which confront counsellors, psychotherapists and other professionals every day. Suitable for both students and practitioners, the books are designed to give a clearer understanding of issues which are often considered complex and contentious.

Books in the series:

Therapy with Children
Debbie Daniels and Peter Jenkins

Pastoral Care & Counselling
Gordon Lynch

Legal Issues in Counselling & Psychotherapy
edited by Peter Jenkins

Dual Relationships in Counselling & Psychotherapy

Exploring the Limits

Gabrielle Syme

SAGE Publications
London • Thousand Oaks • New Delhi

First published 2003

SAGE Publications Ltd
6 Bonhill Street
London EC2A 4PU

SAGE Publications Inc
2455 Teller Road
Thousand Oaks, California 91320

SAGE Publications India Pvt Ltd
B-42, Panchsheel Enclave
Post Box 4109
New Delhi 100 017

British Library Cataloguing in Publication data

A catalogue record for this book is available
from the British Library

ISBN 0 7619 6087 2
ISBN 0 7619 6088 0 (pbk)

Library of Congress Control Number available

Typeset by C&M Digitals (P) Ltd., Chennai, India
Printed in India at Gopsons Papers Ltd, Noida

For Robert, and our children and grandchildren

Contents

List of Tables

List of Exercises

Acknowledgements

This has not been an easy book to write and a number of people have kept me going with their interest and encouragement. The most important, because he has also suffered, is my husband, Robert. When I am writing I am hard to live with and welcome assistance and reject it in equal measure! He has persevered and made a significant contribution to the readability of this book as an interested layperson: if he can understand what I have written, then so will others.

I first became interested in ethical problems when chairing the Association for Student Counselling, and shortly afterwards joined the Standards and Ethics Committee of the British Association for Counselling. It was in this committee that I learned how complex ethical issues can be. I thank BAC(P) for giving me this opportunity. My recent life has been markedly affected by my involvement with the association but I have also got a lot back.

Many colleagues have helped me. The most important is Tim Bond, who first thought I could write this book and encouraged me when I doubted this. He has been a very helpful and constructive series editor and given feedback with the utmost tact. I have enjoyed working with him. Others have read chapters for me. They are Anne Bryant, Dave Mearns, Susie Lendrum and Geoff Pelham. I have greatly appreciated their advice, which has resulted in a much better book.

I have also appreciated the support of the editorial staff at Sage, particularly Alison Poyner who has been patient and understanding throughout. Behind the scenes at different times there have been two secretaries, Jane Hanson and CarolAnn Allan both of whom have patiently tracked down references, made corrections for me and generally sorted out the manuscript when my lack of word-processing skills has created problems.

This book would not have existed without my own therapists and supervisors who have generously shared their knowledge and also helped me sort out why I got stuck at various points when writing this book. I am also grateful to all my clients who have taken risks with me and taught me how to ride the boundaries in a way that is beneficial to them rather than harmful.

Lastly, my family and friends have supported me by being there and always being interested in what I was doing. My family have had far less of my time and attention than they deserve. I would also like to thank Jane Ibberson and Linda Fergusson, who both read some chapters for me.

Again I have valued the input of people without specialist knowledge but with a lot of common sense.

I am really grateful for all the help I have received from those mentioned by name and many others who were there when needed. However, they bear no responsibility for the contents of this book, which are entirely mine.

Introduction

Writing this book has made me acutely aware of boundaries, not only in my own practice but also in our society. In recent years many scandals have been exposed where children in care have been systematically sexually abused by their so-called carers and people in power; priests, teachers and politicians, in particular, have exploited children and women, sexually. It should be stressed that men are also sexually exploited but fewer examples are reported. This under-reporting may be because it occurs less often, but it is equally possible that men are reluctant to report it because of the associated shame. Society is still much more resistant to the idea that men, who are supposed to be macho, could be abused by men or women. Clearly all these scandals are about the crossing of a sexual boundary and the creation of a sexual dual relationship, but other boundaries can also be crossed.

In an article in the *Independent* in 2002 Robert Fisk, a well-respected journalist, discussed the 'boundaries of journalism'. He was expressing his concern that journalists were being asked to become 'policemen' by testifying at the Hague war crimes tribunals. In other words, they were asked to take two roles. Fisk believed that their impartiality was being threatened if they both reported on a conflict and then testified on the part of the prosecutors against particular 'bad guys' in conflicts labelled as war crimes by the West – especially when the West is highly selective about which conflicts and atrocities are selected and which are ignored. Another crossing of boundaries, widely reported as such by the press and radio, occurred when an off-duty prison officer and police constable had lunch with Lord Archer whilst he was on day-release from prison. It seems that therapists' understanding of the importance of boundaries has become a matter of public debate in recent years.

Despite this I have found parts of this book extremely difficult to write. The hardest part consisted of the chapters on non-sexual dual relationships. There were many times when I felt quite paranoid and unsafe, perhaps a mirror of what clients feel when they are challenging therapists and their professional associations about the crossing of boundaries. I certainly felt I was crossing boundaries when I wrote about therapists' love for their clients and the therapeutic use of touch. Of course I knew that these were both taboo topics and that the latter is much more prevalent than people publicly admit. I also knew that privately therapists talk about love, but are terrified they will be accused that this is inappropriate and that they are blind to their sexual and erotic feelings. I think this may be more about how hostile some psychoanalysts and psychotherapists have been to people who practise differently from themselves than a reflection of the reality within counselling. One of my conclusions is that we have a lot to learn and that rigidity in practice does not serve clients well. We have to find a way to take risks that really responds to the conditions in which our clients live and thus help our clients. Rigidity may not harm but it certainly does not help. Of course this is not a licence for doing anything that takes one's fancy: very careful training, good supervision and thoughtful consideration of the rationale for crossing a boundary and the likely impact on clients is necessary. They need to be partners in their therapy and not subjects of experiments.

My training is as a psychodynamic psychotherapist and this is reflected here, although I hope the book will be accessible to all counsellors and psychotherapists. It will be obvious that my style as a therapist is an amalgam of my original training plus all my subsequent life, reading and learning. I have drawn extensively on my own work, with the agreement of clients involved in incidents where it is impossible to disguise the event, even though they have been anonymised. If other examples seem familiar it is because they are accounts of the types of interaction that happen in the everyday life of therapists. Most of my learning has been courtesy of my clients and colleagues, and this is what I am passing on.

1

Boundary Issues are Commonplace: Setting the Limits

Over the last few months while working on this book I have been asked, 'What are you writing about?' My answer has been to explain that what I am examining is why the professional associations of psychologists, counsellors and psychotherapists all insist nowadays that their members avoid dual relationships with their clients. This means that therapists do not mix socially with clients, offer clients another service apart from therapy, purchase services from clients, nor do they offer therapy to another member of a client's family. In other words they only have a professional relationship with a client, and that is as therapist. The standard response to this is, 'Of course! Is there a whole book to be written about that?'

This prohibition of dual relationships is relatively new. The models offered in the early history of psychoanalysis by the 'founders' of the profession reveal a very different picture, with multiple relationships being considered unremarkable. Cooper (1993) suggests that these 'pioneers and heroes' were exploring the analytic relationship 'in order to discover what was possible and what was not', a morality developed gradually in parallel as the impossibilities were discovered. Freud's patients all came from a small, tight-knit, social group in middle-class Vienna so dual relationships were inevitable. He had complicated multiple relationships with all his early associates who were professional colleagues, as well as with friends and his analysands. He also analysed some of his friends' wives. One example is Jones' first wife; although Freud revealed little, Jones did write to Freud enquiring how the analysis of his wife was going and instructing him on what needed to change in his wife (Jacobs, 1992). Freud also analysed his daughter Anna, who subsequently became an analyst in her own right. He crossed many boundaries with his patients that today could have resulted in an appearance before a complaints panel. For instance, he gave patients gifts and financial support, invited the Rat Man for a meal, gave legal advice to some and acted as a matchmaker for two clients (Lazarus and Zur, 2002).

Melanie Klein also had some very complex multiple relationships. She, like Freud, analysed her own children and analysed Jones' second wife and his two children. Indeed Jones invited her to London for this task. Klein later became Winnicott's supervisor and analysed his second wife Clare (Kahr, 1996). To complicate matters further, Winnicott analysed Melanie Klein's son (Jacobs, 1995). Winnicott had multiple relations with Jones, Khan, Milner and Little because he had a relationship with each of them as a colleague and then at least one additional relationship. He analysed Jones' daughter, Margaret Little, Masud Khan and his second wife. Masud Khan edited Winnicott's papers for 20 years from 1950 to 1970 and all the books that Winnicott published during his life-time. In the case of Marion Milner, the Winnicotts took a young woman named 'Susan', whom Alice Winnicott had found in a hospital for nervous diseases, into their home. They then referred her to Marion Milner for psychoanalysis. Throughout the long analysis Winnicott 'not only carried the medical responsibility but was always ready with an illuminating remark on the telephone in moments of crisis' (Milner, 1969). This was not the only time they had a severely disturbed young person and patient of Winnicott living with them (Kahr, 1996). Margaret Little (1985) wrote a very detailed description of her analysis by Winnicott between 1949 and 1955. During the analysis they were both members of the Board and Council of the British Psycho-Analytical Society. Ferenczi went on holiday with some of his patients (Clarkson, 1995). A more recent example of a respected analyst who had dual relationships with her clients is Nina Coltart. In the latter part of her life, when she had semi-retired, some of her long-term clients continued to see her occasionally. She would pick them up by car from the train, give them tea, work with them on their material and then return them to the train.

These relationships were non-sexual and do not appear to have been exploitative or abusive. Jung, however, not only had 'close friendships and love relationships' (Wehr, 1985) with two of his patients Sabrina Spielrein and Toni Wolfe, but almost certainly did have sexual relationships with these women (Rutter, 1990). They later became his students and 'made independent contributions to psychoanalysis and analytical psychology' (Wehr, 1985). Reich married one of his patients and 'saw satisfactory sexual release as a prime goal of therapy' (Marmor, 1972; cited by Russell, 1993). Ferenzi and Rank both had sexual relations with patients or ex-patients (Mann, 1997) as did Perls (Shepard, 1976; cited by Russell, 1993) and Rogers (Clarkson, 1995) and in each of these cases no formal complaint was made and no action taken by either a professional association or the women concerned. It is interesting to compare this with the more recent case of Masud Khan, whose position as a training analyst was terminated by the British Psycho-Analytical Association in 1975 and then in 1988 he was struck off (Cooper, 1993). His termination as a training analyst was related to a number of misdemeanours around boundaries, including a complaint about sexual involvement with a student, although no patient could be persuaded to make a direct complaint (Rayner, 1993). There is indirect evidence that this was not an isolated example of sexual exploitation of a patient. His breaking of the non-sexual boundaries included socialising with patients, introducing them to one another, meddling in their lives and sending them on errands. He was finally struck off for bringing the profession into disrepute. This followed the publication in 1988 of *When Spring Comes*, in which he 'spewed out not only inappropriate self-revelatory information, but also contemptuous anti-semitic venom' (Cooper, 1993). It is clear that Khan's behaviour was extreme and the British Psycho-Analytical Society and his colleagues had been pushed to their limit; however in earlier times it is unlikely that he would have been struck off. By the 1970s the climate of opinion had changed radically; reasons for this change will be explored later.

Outside psychotherapeutic and counselling settings, multiple relationships exist in almost every walk of life and seem to be accepted without comment unless something goes wrong. There is no reason why I should not be friends with my physiotherapist, piano teacher or the local builder, baker or window-cleaner and meet any one of them socially or chat to them if I meet them in the street. None of them has rules from their professional association or employers that prevent social contact. However, the two parties are likely to differentiate in their behaviour and demeanour between the two relationships. If a schoolteacher sends her child to the school at which she teaches there is no rule to prevent this nor to forbid her teaching her child, though she would probably think long and hard before doing so because of its undoubted effect on family relationships. Doctors and dentists will treat family and friends though they would probably not treat very close family except in dire emergencies. There is also no embargo on patients becoming friends. It would not be uncommon for a doctor to have carried out an internal examination of a female patient and then meet her socially at a mutual friend's house a few weeks later. Solicitors often offer preferential rates to family members though they must have any such work, particularly family wills, checked by an impartial colleague.

In many settings multiple relationships are not questioned and are used to get work. This was particularly so when professional bodies prohibited advertising: as a result professionals such as solicitors, physiotherapists, architects, accountants and doctors (pre-1948 and the introduction of the NHS) relied on their social contacts to find clients or patients. Their friends became clients, or vice versa, and in turn they recommended the professional services to others. Even nowadays, with most professional bodies allowing advertising as long as it is accurate, many people still use their friends as a source of work. In this way multiple relationships with clients or patients are both common and useful.

In the 1970s I lectured at a university. I had multiple relationships with my students; teaching them, employing them to baby-sit, arranging and attending at least one social event a term with my tutorial groups, and having one student as a lodger for a whole year. I marked exam papers of all these students at a time when scripts were not anonymous and took part in the examiners' meeting in which their final degree mark was decided. I declared an interest in the case of the student who lodged with me, but was not asked to leave the room during the decision-making and my opinion was actively sought. No one, least of all myself, questioned the propriety of doing this. It was assumed by my colleagues and confirmed by my behaviour that I was a responsible person who acted with integrity and did not abuse either my power or my position of privilege.

For priests, multiple relationships with members of their congregation are inevitable. To conduct their role adequately they will have a spiritual and a pastoral role quite apart from a social role with their church members. Some have eschewed friendship with any parishioners rather than add the further complications that this would entail. Such an approach can have disastrous emotional effects on the priests and their families. I will look specifically at the problem of multiple relationships for priests later in this book.

The professional associations of psychologists, counsellors and psychotherapists have brought in much stricter rules about dual relationships in response to complaints from clients that they have been abused or exploited by a professional helping relationship changing in nature. Countless examples of the potential complications of dual relationships could be drawn from real life situations; perhaps equally pertinent is that this theme has been richly elucidated in twentieth-century fiction and especially in films, revealing the positive as well as the destructive elements of such relationships.

If films and TV programmes are to be believed the development of sexual relationships between therapists and clients is commonplace. The therapist violating the sexual boundary can be male or female. Examples of the former are found in *Basic Instinct* (1992), *Color of Night* (1994), and *The Evening Star* (1996) and of the latter in *Spellbound* (1945), *The Prince of Tides* (1991) and *Mr Jones* (1993). These violations all happen without any suggestion that such behaviour is harmful or unethical and on occasions the implication is that either the client or the therapist was helped by the relationship. Therapists are also portrayed as having affairs or marrying patients the moment therapy ends, or terminating therapy so that a sexual relationship can start. An example of this is in the film *Deconstructing Harry* (1997) directed by Woody Allen, who often makes films portraying therapists who behave unethically. Other examples are *Annie Hall* (1977) and *Husbands and Wives* (1992). In *Husbands and Wives* the male therapist has an affair with his client and then blames her for seducing him! There is no suggestion that therapist must abstain from a sexual relationship with a client.

Some films portray the therapist as a wounded healer who is healed. It is the therapeutic relationship with the client that is the catalyst for the therapist to change – *Good Will Hunting* (1997), *Don Juan DeMarco* (1995) – but in the process the therapist has had two roles: healer for the client and wounded healer helped by the client.

Films also portray confusions between personal and professional roles. *The Prince of Tides* is a particularly interesting example of this because so many boundaries are crossed and different relationships formed between the therapist and her client. For this reason I will look at some parts of this film in some detail. The therapist, Dr Susan Lowenstein, who is played by Barbra Streisand, decides to contact the mother of her suicidal client, Savannah, to find out something about her family because the client is electively mute. When the mother refuses to see the therapist, her son, who is Savannah's twin, Tom Wingo, visits the therapist in her stead. From this point Tom becomes the client and begins to reveal the complex and disturbed childhood he, his sister, and brother Luke, who is now dead, had had. The marriages of both Tom and Lowenstein (as Tom calls her) are rocky. Apart from the therapeutic relationship a personal one grows; they go out for dinner together; she interprets one of his dreams whilst they are dining out; he dines at her house, invited by her husband; he coaches her son in baseball. The relationship develops into a sexual one; they spend a weekend away. At the end of the weekend together they end their relationship and he returns to his wife. They resolve to rebuild their relationship; whether Lowenstein and her husband return to one another is left in doubt.

The other thread of the story concerns Tom's sister who recovers and Lowenstein's son Daniel, who as a result of Tom's intervention is able to stand up to his father and do what he would like with his life. In summary, the boundaries crossed are between professional and personal so that there are several dual relationships. The therapist has a brother and sister as patients. The therapist allows a friendship and then a sexual relationship to develop with a male client. The therapist arranges for her client to offer her son coaching and introduces him to her husband, who then invites him to dinner. At no point in this film is there any suggestion that any of these actions is unethical or harmful; indeed the inference is that all the therapist's actions helped repair her client's marriage. Only one action of Lowenstein is commented upon by Tom as unethical: this is when she throws an inkwell at him. Of course the story and the film would be spoilt by moralising, and it is, as the video sleeve states, 'an emotionally explosive story of profound pain' and 'unlikely passion'. It is a good story.

Another example of complex dual relationships is to be found in *Deconstructing Harry*. The therapist appears to fall in love with her client, Harry, without any attempt by him to seduce her, nor any indication that he is in love with her. She abruptly and prematurely ends the therapy stating, 'The inevitable has happened. I think we should terminate your treatment and give a substantial period of time, and if we both feel the same way I think we could see each other socially'. They subsequently marry and have a child. Harry then proceeds to have affairs with her clients. Again there is no suggestion that the therapist behaved unethically. Is there no adverse comment because sex between a therapist and his or her client makes a good story and what is portrayed is fictional?

It is reasonable to assume that films are representative of the imagination of the culture from which they emerge, and one explanation for therapists being presented as flawed individuals is to manage society's fears of people 'who can read their minds'. Thus therapists are ridiculed as well as shown behaving badly and unethically. None the less it surprises me that on the one hand no adverse comment is made about the multiple relationships and their potential to damage people, nor are there any films in which these crossing of boundaries is portrayed as damaging, and yet everyone expects therapy associations to prohibit dual relationships, whether sexual or non-sexual.

Definitions

These confusions of role and creation of multiple relationships portrayed in the films are called dual relationships in the psychological therapy professions, whether they are dual or multiple. Broadly a dual relationship arises in any situation where a therapist assumes more than one significantly different role either simultaneously or sequentially with a client, supervisee or trainee. These relationships are not necessarily harmful, or unavoidable, but there is always the potential for a conflict of interest and of exploitation of the person seeking help. This makes it critical that whenever there is a possibility of a dual relationship the therapist, who is the person who knows the difficulties that could arise in such relationships, must think about and perhaps discuss with a supervisor the potential conflicts of interest and exploitation before entering into such a relationship.

It is clear from this definition that dual relationships could be sexual or non-sexual. Sexual dual relationships are easier to identify although there is some disagreement over what constitutes sexual activity. This will be discussed later. Examples of non-sexual dual relationships arising for therapists would be counselling a member of one's own family, a friend, a friend's offspring, a colleague, a member of the choir one sings in, or of a church congregation that one belongs to, one's dentist, plumber, or night-school teacher. Equally confusing would be mixing a professional relationship with a social one, such as having a meal with a client or going to a concert, play or film. The potential for conflict and even exploitation in these relationships is obvious, but perhaps less obvious examples of dual relationships are accepting an invitation to a client's wedding; receiving house decoration in lieu of fees; accepting gifts from clients. In each instance a single relationship no longer exists: the friend becomes a client or, vice versa, the client becomes the provider of services. The potential for exploitation is there. It is not only with clients that dual relationships can arise. Counsellors when acting as trainer or supervisor would form a dual relationship with their trainee or supervisee if they simultaneously were also their therapist. Another dual relationship would be acting as both trainer and supervisor to one person. Similarly it is a dual relationship when a counsellor starts a therapeutic relationship with someone within a short period of that person having attended a training course run by the counsellor in question.

All professional bodies prohibit sexual relationships with patients or clients but few give any guidance on non-sexual dual relationships, leaving it to the common sense of their members to handle these with probity. In this respect counselling and psychotherapy are unusual in that in recent years codes of behaviour or practice have been produced with specific guidelines about both sexual and non-sexual dual relations. The rationale for this book is to look at how these professional codes have developed and why some are different from those of other professions. The questions that need to be asked and answered are whether the psychological therapies have introduced something that other professions should be following; or whether they have introduced rules that prevent therapists working creatively and in the best interests of their clients.

2

The Absolute Limit: Sexual Dual Relationships – The Prevalence and Harmful Effects

Sexual dual relationships between therapists and their patients have occurred from the early days of psychoanalysis until the present day. However, until relatively recently little attention was given to the potentially abusive nature of such relationships, or to their prevalence. As society has begun to accept the reality of rape and child sexual abuse it has started to recognise that some people in positions of power and trust sexually abuse their patients, clients, colleagues, students or employees. No profession is immune: doctors, teachers, lawyers, social workers, clergy, therapists, accountants, architects, professional managers, company directors, to name a few, have been perpetrators of such sexual abuse. It is sufficiently prevalent for it to be called 'screwing the payroll' in some building societies and commercial companies. What is shocking is that some of these professionals are expressly working to help people who are ill or troubled and yet can do something that is damaging to the very people they have set out to help, quite apart from damaging their own careers. Though the latter was rarely true until about 20 years ago.

It was not until Peter Rutter started his research in 1984, which culminated in the publication of his book *Sex in the Forbidden Zone* in 1990, that the veil of secrecy started to be lifted. When he started work as a psychiatrist in the 1960s he had believed that the 'presence of impermeable sexual boundaries' was 'a prerequisite to the doctor–patient relationship', and 'doctors or therapists who had sexual relations with their patients were confined to the criminal or lunatic fringe'. It took about 10 years for this 'myth of the beneficent doctor' to be exploded and for him to realise that men who had sex relations with their female patients, clients, church members, students and protégées were not highly disturbed individuals, but able, respectable and respected men who were trusted by the community at large and whose integrity was taken for granted. The American ex-presidents, John F. Kennedy and Bill Clinton are two such men, as is John Major, a former British prime minister. Two events forced Rutter to face the facts. One was that he came within a whisker of having sex with one of his female patients and as it occurred he was aware that part of himself was totally absorbed in the 'sexual intrigue' whilst another part of himself was detached, watching, 'disbelieving that the erotic contact could be imminent', trying to understand what was 'going on inside' and searching for a way to help her. The second event was when he discovered that a psychiatrist who had been a role model for him and whom he had greatly admired, had over the years had sex with many of his female patients (Rutter, 1990).

Whilst this was disturbing enough, he also realised that many professionals whom he knew to be ethical people had ignored these sexual violations and had not reported them. When he started his research in 1984 he found that he was not the first to try and discover the truth. Research had started in the early 1970s. However, such was the denial and collusion that attempts had been made to suppress such work and even threaten researchers with expulsion from their professional associations. This happened to Butler and Zelen (1977; cited by Garrett, 1994) when they merely proposed undertaking research on the incidence of sexual intimacy between psychotherapists and patients. The research data of Forer was actually suppressed (cited by Bouhoutsos, 1983 by Garrett, 1994) whereas in the case of Dahlberg (1970; cited by Rutter, 1990) suppression was tried and failed but he was only able to publish the results in a journal with a very limited circulation. When Rutter (1990) did a literature search in 1984 he found only two books on sex between doctors and patients. One was written by a woman, who had been sexually exploited by a psychiatrist; the other was a book by a psychiatrist advocating the benefits for women of having sex with their male therapist (Shepard, 1971; cited by Rutter, 1990). There was another surprise in store for Rutter. This was that although there were very few articles published about sexual exploitation of women patients by doctors or psychiatrists there were even fewer about sexual contact between men and women in other professions.

What Rutter discovered for the medical profession was equally true for counselling, psychotherapy and psychology: sexual exploitation was known to occur but it was being condoned and no one had any idea what number of practitioners were abusing their clients or patients. It was not until the 1980s in the US that a body of research started to accumulate to quantify what was happening. Research in the UK has lagged considerably behind the US, with the first survey published in 1992. There is now a substantial body of research both in the US and to a lesser extent in the UK. In many instances research has been done with one group of practitioners, and then compared with research on another group of professionals. The results have been sufficiently consistent for it to be reasonable to draw conclusions and extrapolate from one group of professionals to another. What is clear is that members of every profession sexually exploit their clients.

In this chapter I will give some facts and figures and then look at the characteristics of sexual abusers and the abused and the effects on the abused of sexual exploitation by a therapist. I will also discuss the effect of sexual relationships with former clients and trainees. In the following chapter I will look at the theoretical and practical issues related to sexual feelings in the therapist or client.

Facts and figures

All the surveys that I have found try to assess the incidence of sexual abuse of clients by their therapists by questioning therapists rather than surveying the general public or a large group of clients and ex-clients to see how many have been abused by their therapists. It is simpler to survey therapists because they belong to professional associations and will have their names in the public domain as well. Surveying even a sample of the general public would be difficult and expensive. The therapist has an ethical duty to keep the identity of their clients and ex-clients confidential, so clients could be found only by advertising for people willing to take part in such a survey. Russell (1993) did do this and found 40 people who were prepared to talk about sexual abuse by a therapist, but she made a subjective study rather than using a questionnaire and making a statistical analysis. The only other figures available come from professional associations who handle complaints and POPAN (The Prevention of Professional Abuse Network). However, data from these sources could be misleading because it is known that sexual abuse is under-reported by the victims. I will discuss the reasons for this later. This means that all the figures given here are estimates and are likely to be underestimates.

Surveys conducted in the US suggest that 6–7 per cent of psychotherapists have had sexual intercourse with their patients and between 3 and 13 per cent of psychotherapists have had 'erotic' non-intercourse contact with patients (Kardener et al., 1976; Pope et al., 1987; both cited by Garrett, 1994). When this is broken down into gender then about 10 per cent of male therapists have had sexual intercourse with their clients as opposed to 0.6–3 per cent of females. These contrast with a survey which showed that 95 per cent of psychotherapists in the US believed that sex with patients is unethical and about 50 per cent believed that becoming sexually involved with former patients is also unethical (Pope et al., 1987; cited by Garrett, 1994). It is sometimes difficult to compare the research because some surveys were more specific than others. For instance Holroyd and Brodsky (1977; cited by Garrett, 1994) asked their respondents to indicate whether sexual intercourse had occurred whilst psychotherapy was ongoing and found that only 5.5 per cent of men and 0.6 per cent of women admitted to this. However when asked in the same survey whether they had ever had sex with their patients, 8.1 per cent of men and 1 per cent of women therapists indicated that they had done so.

In another survey they conducted later (Holroyd and Brodsky, 1980; cited by Garrett, 1994) they found that 3.2 per cent of those surveyed had had sexual intercourse with patients and another 4.6 per cent had taken part in other types of sexual behaviour.

Garrett conducted a survey in the UK basing her questionnaire on the research conducted in the US (1994). She surveyed 1,000 clinical psychologists and found that 4 per cent admitted to having had sexual contact with current or discharged patients, another 2 per cent had had sexual intercourse with a patient and 2 per cent had had other forms of erotic contact. These levels are lower than those found in the early US studies. However, research done by Pope (1990; cited by Garrett, 1994) suggests that there had been a decline in the incidence of psychotherapist–patient sexual involvement between 1980 and 1990. It is possible that a similar decline had happened in the UK. This may be because in both countries the press began to focus on abuse by professionals. This could have had two effects. A positive effect may have been to reduce the amount of sexual abuse because the general public has been made more aware of the danger, and has been given guidelines on how to make themselves less vulnerable to sexual abuse. The negative effect may have been to make professionals more careful and even more reluctant to answer questionnaires honestly. This is supported by the fact that some people did not answer this question. To compensate for this the respondents were asked how many patients they had treated who had had sexual involvement with previous psychotherapists and what knowledge they had through other sources of psychologists who had had sexual contact with their patients. Both of these questions would inevitably result in overestimates because more than one psychologist could know of the same psychologist abusing clients. Some 22 per cent of clinical psychologists had treated patients abused by an earlier therapist. This therapist may have been a psychotherapist, a counsellor, a social worker, a GP, a psychiatrist, a nurse or a clinical psychologist. About 40 per cent of respondents to the questionnaire knew of psychologists who had had sexual contact with their patients.

A therapist who has had sexual contact with one patient is likely to have sexual contact with others. In the US Gartrell et al. (1986; cited by Garrett, 1994) found that 33 per cent of those they surveyed re-offended and had abused as many as 12 patients. This may well be an under-estimate; data on paedophiles in the UK suggest that they abuse on average 80 children before being caught. I am not suggesting that therapists who abuse their clients are paedophiles but that people perpetrating sexual crimes tend to lie to themselves as well as to others. In her survey of UK psychologists Garrett (1994) asked the respondents how often they had had sexual relations with the patient. The most common response was once (42 per cent); a number of individuals reported having sexual relations with the same patient more than once, with the maximum being ten times. This was another instance when a significant number of respondents who had admitted to sexual contact with patients did not answer the question. In this case it was two-thirds of the respondents.

Garrett found that rather more therapists had sexual contact with past rather than current patients. This is borne out by research in the US (Gartrell et al., 1986; cited by Garrett, 1994). In both the US and UK sexual contact with a current client was as likely to occur during a session as outside sessions.

These surveys indicate that it is mainly adult female women who are sexually abused by male therapists, but a small number of women therapists also sexually abuse their clients, both male and female. The research has tended to assume that the sexual abuse is heterosexual in nature and involves solely vaginal penetration, so no attempt has been made to discover whether the abuse involved oral or anal sex or sado-masochism. Whilst the majority of the abuse seems to be perpetrated by heterosexuals, there is no doubt that homosexuals and lesbians can be perpetrators of sexual exploitation as well. The abuse of men by therapists is almost certainly under-reported, perhaps because it is even harder for men in our society to admit to sexual abuse and to be taken seriously. Male sexual abuse is still a taboo subject and its existence largely denied. We will know the true extent of the problem only when it becomes easier for men to admit to vulnerability in our society. Questionnaires have rarely asked the age of the victim. However in 1989 Bajit and Pope (cited by Garrett, 1994) questioned 81 psychotherapists known to have had sex with child patients and found that 56 per cent of the victims were girls and 44 per cent boys. Their age range was 3 to 17. In a more general survey (Pope and Vetter 1991; cited by Garrett, 1994) 5 per cent of the psychotherapists who had admitted to having sexually abused clients said their victims were children.

Another source of information on the extent of sexual abuse of clients is the professional associations who receive complaints. These associations receive more phone calls about abuse than are actually taken to adjudication. This is partly because the associations receive calls about both members and non-members, but usually restrict themselves to investigating only the behaviour of their own members. Another reason is that the complaints procedures are complicated and difficult for someone with low self-esteem and lacking confidence to follow. This is a major reason for the formation of POPAN, which assists people in making formal complaints. In the year April 2000 to March 2001 the British Association for Counselling and Psychotherapy (BACP) received 158 complaint enquiries, of which 9 related to inappropriate sexual contact or propositioning. In the same time span 60 complaints were in process, of which 5 (8.5 per cent) involved inappropriate sexual contact with a client. The most recent figures for the British Psychological Society (BPS) are for 1999. In this year 79 complaints were resolved; of the 28 complaints received about conduct matters half could be related to sexual exploitation. The total membership of BPS in 1999–2000 was 33,538 compared with 17,500 in BACP, though this latter figure does not include organisational members of BACP, against whom complaints can also be made. The United Kingdom Council for Psychotherapy (UKCP) publishes annual complaints statistics but there is no breakdown by nature of the complaint so no comparison can be made.

Equally valuable are estimates from POPAN. In the year 1999–2000 38 per cent of the cases of abuse reported to them were against counsellors, psychotherapists and psychologists, with most being made against psychotherapists. The categories of abuse ranged through physical, sexual, emotional, financial, emotional and sexual, physical and sexual, and emotional and physical. If one combines the three categories in which at least one component was sexual abuse then 27 per cent of reported cases involved sexual abuse.

Some therapists sexually abuse their clients. Efforts to punish abusers and to be proactive to ensure that sexual abuse does not occur is considerably hampered because it is under-reported by both those who are abused and by professional colleagues who suspect that a therapist is sexually abusing their clients. In Garrett's survey (1994) 41 per cent of cases had not been reported to employers or to any professional association, although almost all of those who indicated in the survey that they had had sexual contact with one or more clients had told at least one other person, such as their manager or supervisor, a colleague, a friend or partner, or their personal psychotherapist. Colleagues are tempted to collude and therefore silently condone sexual abuse of clients rather than make a formal complaint to the relevant professional association. Indeed Greenspan (1994) suggests that many professionals have 'an informal ethic of solidarity'. This takes precedence over their professional codes of ethics, which in a number of professional associations actively encourage the reporting of anyone known to be contravening Codes of Ethics and Practice. For instance BACP's *Ethical Framework for Good Practice in Counselling and Psychotherapy* (2002) states in the section of the code headed 'Responsibilities to all clients':

39. Practitioners have a responsibility to protect clients when they have good reason for believing that other practitioners are placing them at risk of harm.

40. They should raise their concerns with the practitioner concerned in the first instance, unless it is inappropriate to do so. If the matter cannot be resolved, they should review the grounds for their concern and the evidence available to them and, when appropriate, raise their concerns with the practitioner's manager, agency or professional body.

Rutter (1990) suggests that male therapists do not report their male colleagues because they secretly harbour fantasies of having 'forbidden' sex and envy men who have managed to do so. Perhaps it is also difficult for therapists, whether male or female, because they think they are being disloyal and feel as if they are betraying a fellow practitioner. This may be especially so because therapists try to be non-judgmental and accepting of others' behaviour and would therefore resist accusing someone of malpractice. In this situation it would be wise to talk over the dilemmas with someone of maturity and wisdom, possibly one's therapist or supervisor, provided they are impartial. If a therapist does not report suspected sexual abuse of a client by a fellow therapist this is false loyalty and a derogation of their duty of care to the general public.

Characteristics of abusers and the abused

Pope (1990) and Gutheil (1991), who are both cited by Garrett (1994), observed that much of the early research tended to identify what puts certain women at risk of sexual exploitation by a therapist, or any other powerful male for that matter, and then almost by sleight of hand shift the blame from the therapists to the women. In this type of explanation the vulnerable woman idealises and worships the man, who under the duress of such powerful transference and countertransference succumbs to the pressure; in other words is seduced by the woman. Whilst certain women would want to seduce a man, it has to be clear that any therapist who is seduced sexually exploits his client and this act is always abusive. It is only with this in mind that I am comfortable in looking at whether there are life stories and psychological characteristics of some women that make them vulnerable to sexual exploitation; but first, even though this research was conducted later, I want to look at the psychological profile of therapists who sexually exploit their clients. Much of what follows can be found in more detail in publications by Rutter (1990), Garrett (1994) and Hetherington (2000).

The abuser

The first person to explore the characteristics of therapists who sexually exploit their clients was Dahlberg (1970; cited by Rutter, 1990). His report was based on psychotherapists whom he treated after they had had sexual relationships with patients. They were all men, over 40 and 10–15 years older than their patients. There was evidence that some were having difficulty in their marriage and the men were unusually shy, withdrawn, introspective, intellectual, passive and studious. Dahlberg postulated that this made them unpopular with women and therefore vulnerable when patients were attracted to them. He suggested that the psychotherapist is acting out a fantasy of 'being young, attractive and having beautiful girls throwing themselves at you without having to take the chance of being rejected by being the one to make the first move'. He further suggests that this is an acting out of a fantasy of male omnipotence. Strean (1993; cited by Hetherington, 2000) from his research with therapists who had sex with their clients confirmed most of Dahlberg's factual observations, but added that the men were of some standing professionally, dissatisfied with their love relationships, over-involved in work, lonely and needy. Despite difficulty in personal relationships with women these men had a preponderance of female clients (Gabbard, 1989; Sussman, 1992; cited by Hetherington, 2000). Strean (1993) also found that bisexuality was a common characteristic of therapists who sexually exploited their clients. Hetherington suggests that these therapists have an 'unstable sexual identity' caused by a lack of maternal responsiveness to them when children. This would have led to a yearning for closeness and possibly a regression to homosexual preoccupations and a resultant anxiety around their sexuality, preventing them enjoying close reciprocal relationships as teenagers or adults. The existence of a female client with a strong erotic transference can be very reassuring to someone who has difficulty in creating close and meaningful relationships in his private life. In these circumstances the temptation to make the sexual relationship real can be too great.

There is some evidence, though this is not corroborated by further studies, that therapists who have had personal therapy are more likely to sexually abuse their clients (Gartrell et al., 1986; cited by Garrett, 1994), as are those therapists who had sexual contact with their trainers, who may have been supervisors, psychotherapists or teachers (Pope et al., 1986; cited by Garrett, 1994). The former may seem surprising, but is less so when one knows that there is little evidence that therapy, however extensive, can prevent further abusive acts; 'once an abuser always an abuser' is often said. The research that has been done does not address the reasons why a person went into therapy. It would need to do so if a definitive statement is to be made about whether therapists who have had therapy are more likely to abuse their clients. The research is also hard to interpret without some evidence of efficacy of therapy. It is possible to have had extensive periods of therapy and still not to get to the root of the psychopathology. For these two reasons it is necessary to maintain an open mind on whether there is a correlation between having received therapy and sexually abusing clients. It may be a spurious connection. The correlation between having had sexual contact with one's trainer and sexually abusing one's clients is less surprising as there has been inappropriate modelling during training (Pope et al., 1986; cited by Garrett, 1994).

Another line of research has been to analyse the personality of therapists who sexually abuse their patients. Unsurprisingly sex with a client fulfils needs in their own psychic lives (Fine, 1982 and Gartrell et al., 1986; cited by Hetherington, 2000). Gonsoriek (1987; cited by Garrett, 1994) found that the psychotherapists accused of abusing clients sexually made up a diverse group. Some were apparently psychologically healthy, although shy and lonely, but others were mildly neurotic, severely neurotic, suffered from impulsive, sociopathic or narcissistic character disorders, or had psychotic or borderline personalities. In another study Butler and Zelen (1977; cited by Garrett, 1994) interviewed male psychologists and psychiatrists who had sexually abused patients. Over half (60 per cent) saw themselves in a paternalistic role with a submissive and passive patient; 15 per cent described themselves as domineering and controlling.

Most studies on therapists making sexual contact with a patient suggest that the motivation is to do with power needs (Bouhoutsos, 1983; cited by Garrett, 1994). In a more detailed study Sonne and Pope (1991; cited by Garrett, 1994) suggested that the act involved anger, power and sadism. The sexual abuse therefore is an angry attack involving a metaphorical battering of the patient by the abuser, who may even deceive himself into believing that it is being done for the patient's good. There is an abuse of power by someone often of an authoritarian nature, perhaps attracted to the very vulnerable and damaged client or even the physically immobile client. Finally there is a sadistic attack where pleasure is derived from causing pain and sexual humiliation. Needless to say any perpetrator is putting his needs before those of the patient (Averill et al., 1989; cited by Garrett, 1994). Claman (1987; cited by Garrett, 1994) postulates that this is because many sexually abusive therapists have a narcissistic disturbance of the self, harbouring from their childhood unfulfilled longings to be mirrored and needs to merge. Both these yearnings are fulfilled by sexual contact with a patient. This in turn would suggest the need for an in-depth psychoanalysis to deal with such early psychological damage – a commitment that few people are willing to undertake or are prepared to afford.

Rutter (1990) as a Jungian offers explanations from analytical psychology of why sexual exploitation occurs. He suggests that exploitative sex arises as a result of unconscious efforts to assuage masculine psychological woundedness. These wounds arise partly from cultural attitudes and also from dysfunctional relationships with either or both parents. Firstly Western cultures tend to place men in a vicious circle, which is hard to break. Men are taught to be macho and deny weakness, illness and vulnerability. This denial of elements of their self results in severe inner woundedness, which can only be healed by the recognition of their vulnerability, which is itself taboo. The psychological wounds are manifest in symptoms such as anxiety, depression, obsessive and destructive behaviour. Fantasies of sexual merger with a woman often offer some assuagement of the inner damage. These fantasies make men very vulnerable in a society that neither understands nor values fantasies but instead encourages men to act them out with 'real' women. Sexual fantasy is a normal and essential way for a man to explore his feminine self, because the female of his inner world carries his split-off qualities of receptivity, sensitivity, capacity to nurture, non-competitiveness, inner-directedness and vulnerability, which are often labelled as feminine and therefore unacceptable in the macho male of Western cultures.

Other psychological wounds leading to crossing the sexual boundaries arise because it is rare for a man to have been intimate with his father: to have learned from his father about his vulnerabilities, conflicts, doubts and failures and about his sexual or emotional feelings. Without a guide from his father a man does not learn to contain his sexual needs but will act them out and will also have an over-dependence on women for intimacy. There are other wounds that occur as a result of a dysfunctional relationship between a man and his mother, again resulting is inappropriate sexual boundaries and a crossing of the forbidden zone. Typically these arise when a man has been too merged with his mother and therefore unable to separate from her; or when a man has been deprived of closeness by a cold and distant mother; or when a man repeats the victimisation of women that he saw his mother enduring (Rutter, 1990).

A therapist with any of the psychological wounds mentioned puts himself and his female patient in a very unsafe place, behind the closed doors of the consulting room. The patient is there because she is vulnerable and she can become merged with the vulnerable woman of the male therapist's fantasy. This may result in the therapist 'project[ing] into her body and spirit the "feminine" feeling potential and mystery that he has shut himself off from' (Rutter, 1990). He will be drawn to his female patient for healing and intimacy and will be tempted to act out his fantasy instead of containing it within himself.

The abused

The information on the characteristics of clients who are sexually exploited by their therapists relates solely to adult women. There are two reasons for this. Firstly the vast majority of clients who are sexually exploited by their therapists are adult women. Secondly, until recently it has been largely ignored that men and children can be, and have been, sexually abused by female or male therapists. The first piece of research by Belote is cited by Bouhoutos (1983; cited by Garrett, 1994). The female clients who were abused sexually were vulnerable, and had a poor self-image, low self-actualisation and little acceptance of their own aggression. Averill et al. (1989) and Gutheil (1989) (both cited by Garrett, 1994) found that sexual violations are most likely to occur with patients who have borderline personality disorders and who have been in long-term therapy. In one survey Pope and Vetter (1991; cited by Garrett, 1994) found that there was a history of childhood sexual abuse (32 per cent) and/or rape (10 per cent). Pope and Bouhoutros (1986; cited by Garrett, 1994) suggested that women clients who may be very stressed but are basically psychologically healthy are at low risk of being sexually abused by their male therapists. Those women who have a history of relationship problems and may also have a personality disorder are more at risk; and those who are at high risk have a history of hospitalisation, suicide attempts, major psychiatric illness and substance abuse. All these characteristics of the high-risk group are also known to be common in women who have been sexually abused in childhood. Women who have already been sexually abused by one therapist are very vulnerable to sexual abuse by another (Folman, 1991; Gartrell et al., 1987; cited by Garrett, 1994).

An example of the repeat pattern in which women who are sexually assaulted as children are vulnerable to the same type of assault from therapists is given by the writer Elizabeth Jane Howard. In her autobiography *Slipstream, A Memoir* (2002), she writes of how when she was a 14-year-old her father suddenly grabbed her breasts and almost stifled her with what she later discovered was a French kiss. This recurred until she learnt to never be alone with him. She describes how frightened and betrayed she felt and writes of feeling too ashamed to tell anyone. When she was 21 she sought help from a Freudian psychiatrist because she knew she was in danger of having yet another affair and wanted help to avoid it. One afternoon she arrived for a session to find 'a plate of cakes and a small bottle of wine on the table between' them 'for a little celebration'. At the end of the session he suddenly lunged at her and 'enclosed her in vice-like grip' saying, 'I love and adore you and want you.' She managed to push him off and rushed out. As she left she fleetingly recalled the first time her father had sexually attacked her but 'pushed it down'. She also felt frightened and betrayed just as she had six years earlier.

Rutter (1990), again writing from a Jungian perspective, suggests that when a woman enters therapy with a powerful man psychological wounds are opened. He categorises these wounds into four groups. They result from

1 overt sexual or psychological invasion in childhood (as in the case of Elizabeth Jane Howard);
2 profound childhood aloneness so any attention is welcome;
3 exploited compassion, so that the victim automatically takes care of any wounded person;
4 devalued potential in the world outside the home.

Rutter found that many of the women he interviewed both 'knew' the initial approaches were seductive and at the same time denied this, seeing it only as non-sexual caring and a recognition of their 'specialness'. Of course, this is the woman's need to be special, being exploited by the therapist. The women also found they were unable to refuse the sexual advances even when these went against their own moral code. They describe feelings of being 'repulsed' or 'degraded' even as they begin the sexually exploitative relationship and cannot act on them. It often takes years before this revulsion can be acted upon and the women feel strong enough to disengage from the relationship or initiate a formal complaint about the abuse. Indeed many never feel strong enough to do so, which is a major reason why sexual abuse is under-reported. Rutter suggests that the reasons for this are that the emotional currents in such a situation are overwhelming because the relationship has many parent–child qualities, which many would insist were necessary to the therapeutic relationship. Without any basis in reality the 'child' feels s/he will die if the parent is not happy. An unloved and lonely person is particularly vulnerable to this feeling and will do almost anything to please the parent and maintain the relationship. This pattern is familiar to anyone working with abused children. If they feel abandoned or unloved they will go to great lengths to try to win back the love and attention of their parents – even parents who have severely abused them emotionally, physically or sexually. It is clear from this that the childlike part of these women is aroused and the agreement or acquiescence to the sexual intercourse is not 'adult' consent.

Obviously these women are very vulnerable, which makes their sexual exploitation by therapists even more serious. Even if a woman is flirtatious and encourages sexual overtures these must be resisted and understood as part of the transference to be interpreted and not acted upon. Therapists must never cross the boundary into the forbidden zone: if they do so the women are harmed even more.

Effects of sexual exploitation by a therapist

The only reliable information on the effects of sexual abuse must be from the abused themselves or from therapists who have not sexually abused any clients and have worked with women who have been sexually exploited by a previous therapist. Therapists who have had sex with a client often rationalise the act by saying it did no harm or even had a positive effect. In one survey of 34 therapists (Taylor and Wagner, 1976; cited by Garrett, 1994), 21 per cent said that psychotherapist–patient sex had a positive effect, balanced against the remainder stating that the effects were negative or mixed. A more recent survey in the US of psychologists who had treated patients who had been sexually intimate with a previous psychotherapist (Pope and Vetter, 1991; cited by Garrett, 1994) found that harm had occurred in 90 per cent of cases. Harm had also occurred in 80 per cent of cases of people who had had a sexual contact with their therapist after the ending of the therapeutic relationship.

Pope and Bouhoutos (1986; cited by Garrett, 1994) have described the severe effects of having sexual contact with one's therapist as a syndrome in its own right, which they call therapist–patient sex syndrome. Its characteristics are drawn from the observations of number of pieces of research, and are:

- ambivalence and guilt;
- feelings of isolation and emptiness;
- cognitive dysfunction;
- identity and boundary disturbance;
- an inability to trust;
- sexual confusion;
- lability of mood and suppressed rage;
- increased suicidal risk;
- an increase in the patients' symptoms: hospitalisation is frequently necessary;
- development of disturbances in interpersonal relationships.

Rutter (1990) from his own interviews with women sexually abused by men in power adds that a number of women have been unable to conceive. He interprets this as the death of hope, which has profound physiological effects as well as causing emotional and psychological damage.

There is no better way to illustrate the effects than to quote from an abused woman. There are many to choose from. The example that follows is from Rutter's book *Sex in the Forbidden Zone* (1990). It is an account given by a psychologist, Patricia Elmont. She was 26, had two children and was feeling very depressed, having recently moved with her husband to a new community a long way away from where she had grown up. This depression was what led her to seek psychotherapy. At the start of therapy her hope, encouraged by her therapist Dr Thomas Stuben, was that her pent-up energy could be redirected into something creative. Instead it was diverted into the relationship with him.

> Thomas excited me immediately with his ideas and intellect. I had a tremendous passion for religious understanding, but no place to put it. I knew this was the real source of my depression. He was very supportive of me. In fact, he was the first man who really seemed excited by my mind, rather than my body. Although I knew he was carrying tremendous spiritual power for me, I couldn't separate it from the sexual. I was so excited by what was going on that I started developing erotic fantasies about him. (1990: 125)

She assumed these erotic feelings were not dangerous because she trusted that Dr Stuben would not respond to them because he was a therapist and bound by professional ethics. Imagine her surprise when the professional boundaries started to be blurred when he invited her to a party at his house and then suggested that she drive him to a lecture he was giving. Her feelings became even more confused when he backed away from the latter suggestion giving as a reason that 'We might not be able to keep our hands off each other.' This revelation that he found her sexually attractive and was tempted to seduce her was devastating as she was already unclear about the boundary between 'sexual and non-sexual passion'. His sexually explicit comment was tantalising because it increased her sexual fantasising, but tormenting because she knew that it would be wrong to have sex with him.

Just as she suspected, shortly afterwards he suggested they have sexual intercourse during a therapy session.

> I felt incapable of doing anything that might disappoint him. So of course I couldn't say no. It never occurred to me to say no. I was horribly lonely and depressed, and by now I had become totally dependent on him for any chance of expressing myself. (1990: 126)

For a year they had sexual intercourse in his office twice weekly during therapy sessions. For the entire time she felt compelled to keep the secret and incapable of doing anything that would end the relationship. It only stopped when her husband was transferred to another area.

She felt she could not possibly enter another therapeutic relationship, although she needed to do so, because of what had happened in the previous one. Her marriage became increasingly unstable and finally broke up after she confessed to having had a sexual relationship with her former therapist. She did subsequently remarry but is still aware of the damage it did to her.

> I felt very depressed each time we had sex. But I'm not sure, after all this time, that I've really looked at how damaging that sexual relationship was. At its best, therapy can help someone discover her inner passion and help channel it into meaningful life's work. He destroyed that possibility in me for a very long time. I'm a pretty tough person. I didn't die from it, and I have for the most part recovered. But he took at least ten years of my life away from me that I had to devote to getting over the damage. It was really evil. (1990: 127)

This account illustrates how when a client loses their sense of boundaries they are totally dependent on the therapist to hold them clearly and firmly. If a therapist's own fantasy life is stimulated by an involvement with a vulnerable woman it is critical that he is very vigilant and discusses what is happening with a supervisor or senior colleague to ensure that the boundary is not crossed. It also shows the profoundly ambivalent feelings a client experiences even as the abuse is taking place, and also the long-lasting effects, which can persist for life, following this type of abuse. It is common for women to say that years of their lives were stolen and lost. They have to grieve for this on top of all the other emotional work they need to undertake after such an abusive experience. Finally it illustrates the small ways in which the boundaries are eroded immediately preceding the crossing of the boundary from a professional relationship to an abusive sexual relationship. Other accounts can be found in Russell's book, *Out of Bounds* (1993).

Sexual relationships with former clients

It has already been mentioned that rather more therapists admit to having had sex with former than with current clients. On occasions the therapy relationship has been stopped so that a sexual relationship can be started and thus accusations of misconduct can be avoided. This devious behaviour happens because some codes of ethics only ban sexual contact and exploitation of clients who are in therapy and have no strictures about past clients. One piece of research by Pope and Venner (1991; cited by Garrett, 1994) found that psychotherapists working with people who had been sexually exploited by their therapist after the end of therapy estimated that 80 per cent of the clients had been harmed. Another survey by Butler and Zelen (1977; cited by Garrett, 1994) of psychotherapists who had had sexual contact with their clients concluded that 'it was not a therapeutic relationship for either patient or therapist'.

The recognition of the mutual harm – but especially the harm to the client – and the knowledge that some therapists had terminated therapy with a client so that they could have a sexual relationship with them, led BAC to introduce a clause into their 1993 *Code of Ethics and Practice for Counsellors* about relationships with former clients. This concern can also be found in the *Ethical Framework for Good Practice in Counselling and Psychotherapy* (BACP, 2002). The approach and advice in the 1993 *Code of Ethics* cannot be bettered and therefore I am quoting it:

> Counsellors remain accountable for relationships with former clients and must exercise caution over entering into friendships, business relationships, sexual relationships, training and any other relationships. Any changes in relationship must be discussed in counselling supervision. The decision about change(s) in relationship with former clients should take into account whether the issues and power dynamics present during the counselling relationship have been resolved and properly ended.

There is some evidence that in many cases the power dynamics were not resolved nor the counselling relationship properly ended, in that very few of the sexual relationships lasted (Garrett, 1994). In her survey (1994) 67 per cent of psychotherapists said they were no longer in contact with the patient with whom they had most recently had a sexual relationship and in only 8 per cent of cases were the therapist and client married or in a committed relationship. It is for this reason that a number of therapeutic organisations prohibit sex with all former clients. In these associations, most of which are from the psychoanalytic end of the spectrum of modalities, the transference is never resolved and therefore the power inequalities remain. However, I have met a few couples who originally met when one was a client and the other the therapist and who have been in a committed relationship for many years. This is evidence that it is possible for a therapeutic relationship to change to a personal and sexual one without harm to either party. Of course since there will be some transference in every relationship there is no reason why some relationships that move from therapeutic to personal should not last. Nevertheless, there is sufficient evidence of the harmful effects to indicate that a change of relationship should only be undertaken with extreme caution.

Sexual relationships with trainees

There has been very little research on the number of senior practitioners in training roles as teachers, therapists or supervisors who have had sexual contact with their trainees. In Garrett's survey in the UK (1994) 5 per cent of psychologists admitted to having had sexual contact with students to whom they were lecturing or whose work they were supervising. Nine per cent of respondents had had sexual contact as undergraduates with their lecturer or tutor and 8 per cent had had sexual contact whilst trainee clinical psychologists with their lecturer, supervisor or tutor. Not all trainee clinical psychologists had had personal therapy but 2 per cent of those who had done so had had some sexual involvement with their psychotherapist.

This should never have happened, but it is doubly serious because, as was mentioned earlier, there is some evidence that those therapists who had sexual contact with their trainers during their training are more likely to sexually abuse their clients. This is confirmed by a study of Pope et al. (1986; cited by Garrett, 1994) who found that amongst a small group of women therapists who had had sexual contact with their clients, 23 per cent had sexual contact with their trainers, whereas only 6 per cent had not. In this study the group of men who had sexually abused clients was too small for any significant conclusion to be drawn. However there is considerable evidence from all walks of life that those who are abused are more likely to be abused again or become abusers. For this reason alone senior members of the profession who sexually abuse their trainees, supervisees and clients must be brought to book and their right to practise removed. Unfortunately until registration is implemented this cannot happen, even though their membership of their professional association can be terminated.

In the next chapter I will look at the significance of erotic feelings for both the therapist and client and at how these can be used to understand the client and for the benefit of the therapeutic relationship. I will also look at the warning signals for both therapist and client that boundaries are in danger of being crossed and strategies that can be used to prevent this happening.

3

The Significance of Sexual Feelings in the Therapeutic Relationship

Therapy, particularly when it is long-term, is an intimate and passionate, though professional, relationship. It involves the emotional engagement of the client and the therapist's love and empathy. Hirsch and Kessel (1988) suggest that therapists frequently feel a mature, adult-to-adult love of their clients, which enhances the work. They stress that these feelings must be related to mature attitudes and not to self-gratifying and narcissistic ones. Maslow (1962) grappling somewhat earlier with the same problem describes the mature love as B-love as opposed to D-love. The former offers love for the being of the other person and the latter expects the other to be a source of love. This he calls deficiency love. In other words the therapist is not offering love in order to be loved, even adored, by the client, but the love is what enables the transformation to take place. Indeed, in a letter to Jung, Freud writes, 'essentially, one might say, the cure is effected by love'. For many, successful therapy will give them the capacity to love. To quote Mann (1997): 'There can be only one way to love and that is through love.' Despite Freud's statement made in 1906 (McGuire, 1974; cited by Mann, 1997), love is a taboo subject (Lear, 1990; cited by Mann, 1997). Perhaps this is illustrated by Maslow's and others' endeavours to define the mature love needed by a therapist for a client.

My experience is that many therapists are very reluctant to talk about love of their clients publicly, but will often do so privately in a supervision session. This reluctance may be because therapists fear that they will be misunderstood and accused of crossing sexual boundaries. Perhaps also a supervisor is the one person a therapist feels safe enough with to talk of their deep feelings and have them authenticated. As Mann (1997) states, the cure effected by love is neither 'cure by love' as suggested by Ferenczi (1926, cited by Mann, 1977), nor a cure through a 'corrective emotional experience' as advocated by Alexander (1950, cited by Mann, 1997). By this Alexander meant that the therapist should behave in ways that are opposite to those of the parents. The cure is effected by the therapist accepting and understanding all the feelings of a client, including the love and erotic feelings, to liberate the 'optimum range of [the client's] emotional experiences, so that [s/he] can form more satisfactory and loving relationships outside therapy' (Mann, 1997). Gerrard (1996) goes even further, suggesting that 'it is only when a patient can arouse our deepest feelings (not empathy) that we can really hope for a truly positive outcome from our work'.

Erotic transference and countertransference

This fear of talking about love seems to go hand in hand with fear of mentioning the erotic feelings clients often have for therapists, and vice versa; these are known as erotic transference and countertransference respectively. There is a long history behind this which is presented in some detail by several authors including Hirsch and Kessel (1988), Welles and Wrye (1991) and Mann (1997, 1999). The earliest account of erotic transference and countertransference is found in the first paper by Freud and Breuer (1895). This is the account of the treatment of Anna O. by Breuer twice a day for 18 months. The treatment came to an abrupt end for reasons that are not made clear in the case study. Freud later revealed to Jones that the abrupt ending happened because Breuer became very frightened when he realised he could not get Anna O. out of his mind. He was so absorbed by her that he was talking about her endlessly to his wife, who became increasingly jealous and morose. Breuer saw that his marriage was in danger and therefore stopped the analysis on the pretext that Anna O. was much better. In fact she was not better and Breuer was called out that night because she was in the throes of a hysterical childbirth. He calmed her down using hypnosis and then left, taking his wife on a second honeymoon. With hindsight it is clear that Anna O.'s hysterical childbirth was the logical conclusion to an unrecognised and unanalysed erotic transference. Equally, Breuer's inability to get her out of his mind was due to an erotic countertransference. Breuer referred Anna O. to Freud and as a consequence of his work with her the idea of transference was postulated.

Freud's first paper about erotic transference was written in 1915 and entitled 'Observations on Transference Love'. For Freud love and the erotic were synonymous. He wrote the paper because the reputation of psychoanalysis was being damaged by several psychoanalysts having sex with their patients. The power of the erotic feelings in the analytic relationship was such that analysts were acting on them rather than analysing them. Freud made an important observation: that patients fall in love with their analysts because of the analytic situation and not because of the personality of the analyst. He initially understood the erotic transference as a resistance which interferes with therapy, because it makes the patient lose interest in understanding and also attempts to reduce the analyst's authority by making him a mere lover. The rule of abstinence – which means maintaining a 'blank screen' and being emotionally detached, not touching a client and sitting out of sight of the client – was a deliberate attempt to ensure that the transference love, which he believed was different from normal love, was not induced nor maintained by the analyst's behaviour. Instead the erotic transference comes from the patient's unconscious and will persist until the analytic task is complete, with the love traced back to its unconscious infantile origins and made conscious.

Nowadays many therapists do not see transference love as different from normal love, nor do they see the erotic transference as negative. When people are in love they want to change for their lover, and to be lovable, known and understood by their lover; thus the love is a force for change. It is suggested that similarly the erotic transference is a positive force in a therapeutic relationship and is potentially transformational, resulting in emotional growth. Therefore 'the emergence of the erotic transference signifies the patient's deepest wish for growth' (Mann, 1997). This does not give therapists permission to actively induce the erotic transference, which would be a seduction. The erotic transference will appear if therapists are not frightened of these feelings and therefore consciously suppress them or unconsciously encourage repression in both themselves and their patients.

Breuer almost certainly had a very strong erotic countertransference to Anna O. and was obviously very frightened by what had happened to him. It may well be that Freud also had experiences of erotic countertransference and developed all the procedures commonly used by analysts to this day not only to ensure that analysts did not unnecessarily provoke sexual attraction and the erotic transference, but also to help him manage his 'troublesome erotic countertransference' (Schachter, 1994; cited by Mann, 1997). Initially Freud did touch his patients, stroking their head and neck. He also encouraged them to touch him (Breuer and Freud, 1895), but later the placing of the analyst's chair behind the couch was done to discourage patients from embracing their analyst. Most of Freud's theoretical explanations were developed to manage the situations in which he found himself. Freud also believed that a properly analysed therapist would have no countertransference feelings and if they existed they were manifestations of an unresolved neurosis of the therapist. This led to therapists being very worried if they had any feelings towards their patients and seeking more therapy for themselves. It is only in the last 50 years, starting with a paper by Paula Heimann (1950), that the value of the therapist's countertransference has been recognised as a cue to the client's internal world and this is true for all feelings, including erotic ones. The history of this changing understanding of countertransference can be found in a number of papers: particularly clear expositions can be found in Gabbard (1995), Jacobs (1999) and Hinshelwood (1999).

There has been a huge change in the profession since 1990, following from the acceptance that the therapist's countertransference is an important tool in the therapy and that therefore an erotic countertransference is something to think about in the pursuit of understanding and helping the client rather than to banish. Mann (1997) has found that therapists attending his workshops on 'Working with the erotic transference and countertransference' are acknowledging that in some of their cases erotic transference or countertransference or both happen. In 1986 Pope and Bouhoutsos (cited by Garrett, 1994) found in a survey of therapists in the US that 95 per cent of men in private practice and 76 per cent of women felt sexual attraction to at least one client. In a survey of clinical psychologists conducted by Garrett (1994) in the UK 56 per cent of respondents reported being sexually attracted to a client, with this being more likely in the male psychologists. This is borne out by my own experience, both personally and as a supervisor. Whereas male therapists often report having an erotic countertransference to some of their female clients I have never had an erotic countertransference to any of my male or female clients and nor have any of my female supervisees. It is also rare for a woman client, though common for a male client, to have an erotic transference to a female therapist. Susie Orbach makes a similar observation in *The Impossibility of Sex* (1999). She goes on to question whether the erotic is so deeply repressed in women that it fails to emerge. If it is not repressed then do the theories about infant sexuality and mother–child, and mother–daughter sexuality need revision? Her suggestion, which is also as attempt to explain why many women find that their erotic feelings disappear in long-term relationships, is that for a variety of reasons the 'erotic is not woven into [woman's] experience of self and her experience of mothering an infant'. Thus although the infant has the capacity to use the erotic as a 'potential form of expression', a mother's dissociation from her eroticism might leave both the infant's and the child's sexuality dormant. It would then be dormant in any relationship that bears a likeness to the maternal dyad. Two such situations are in the dyad of therapist and client and in close sexual relationships. To support this, I found that I loved my newborn children with an intensity I have only felt when 'in love' with a man. I was aroused erotically, as I felt intense uterine contractions the first time they suckled; after that, breast-feeding was highly pleasurable but I did not have erotic feelings.

Joy Schaverien (1997) also observes that there are few reports by women therapists of their erotic countertransference. Her theoretical explanation of this phenomenon is quite different from Susie Orbach's. She suggests that it may be more acceptable to a female therapist to view her role in maternal terms rather than as that of a potential lover. She cites one case of her own where she realised in retrospect, after a male client had left therapy abruptly and unexpectedly, that she had unconsciously denied her sexual attraction to him and instead had interpreted his desire for her to see him as attractive as a wish for her to see the little boy. Schaverien suggests that her unconscious denial of her attraction to the client repeated his childhood experience of being belittled by his mother, who could not manage her incestuous feelings for her adolescent son, except by denial. In retrospect she realised that if she had been able to tell him that she found him attractive but that a sexual relationship was taboo, and that she was not frightened by his erotic transference to her, then he would not have abruptly terminated therapy. Indeed she goes on to suggest that an important question for therapists to ask themselves is 'Why am I not aroused by this person?'

One result of the changed attitudes to erotic transference and counter-transference is first of all to enable therapists to talk more openly about their sexual feelings, both in workshops and in supervision, so that these feelings can be thought about and an understanding gained about what they might signify. This has also resulted in many more papers, some theo-retical and others practical, about the issues. I have cited a number in this chapter. A particularly interesting paper by two female psychoanalysts, Welles and Wrye (1991), brings together the erotic transference and countertransference and offers a further explanation for why the erotic countertransference is often not felt by therapists. In common with a number of other analysts they believe that 'hatred and aggressive drives are often concealed behind love and sexual need'. They suggest that a 'sensual erotic contact between the mother and the baby' is recreated in the maternal erotic transference and the maternal erotic countertrans-ference and that 'this bodily-oriented transference–countertransference' is especially important because it is one way, perhaps the only way, that preverbal experiences of both concrete loving and hateful erotic wishes can be conveyed to the therapist.

They focus on the female therapist, suggesting that it is even more difficult for women than men to identify themselves with debased projec-tions, such as fat, smelly prostitute (an example given by Torras de Bea, 1987; cited by Welles and Wrye, 1991), which are a product of a man's hatred, in a society where women are still belittled and vilified in many ways. Women therapists may also fear 'being blamed for causing arousal in the man, or of being seen as needy and seductive' (Schaverien, 1997) in a society where a rapist's defence can still be that the woman seduced him. This fear may well result in 'powerful and primitive wishes and defences' in the female analyst which may lead to a blocking of her awareness of the maternal erotic countertransference.

Welles and Wrye suggest three common countertransference constel-lations, which mask the maternal erotic countertransference. The first constellation is the 'need to infantilise the patient to perpetuate exces-sively a mother–baby fusion' and thus avoid conflict and separateness and inhibit the maturation of the client. The second one is seen in 'the analyst's impulse to rebirth and remake the patient'. This results in a constant focus on the client's dependency needs rather than on their erotic and aggressive feelings. The third form 'stems from the analyst's inability or defensive refusal to participate in an erotically charged interaction' and results in the therapist feeling dead, bored, uninvolved and lacking in creative responses. If these three responses can be recognised as the result of blocked maternal erotic countertransference then the client's erotic transference can be recognised and understood first by the therapist and then by the client so emotional growth can occur. Welles and Wrye believe that this interplay of the erotic transference of the client and the erotic countertransference of the therapist is essential for a transformation to take place in therapy.

Welles and Wrye, Schaverien and Orbach are all trying to understand why few female therapists report erotic countertransference feelings. The question that still needs to be answered is whether such feelings are absent because they are being blocked for defensive reasons in women therapists and thus a way has to be found to bring them to awareness, or whether this is a normal developmental difference between men and women.

Despite the increased discussion of erotic transference and counter-transference there is still very little discussion of homoerotic transference or countertransference and no surveys to discover their incidence. This may well be because it is still taboo to admit to such feelings, which is not surprising when a number of psychoanalytic trainings will not accept gay candidates as trainees. It is also likely that some therapists who have homoerotic feelings suppress them because they are frightening. Others will have no homoerotic feelings because they have been totally repressed. One group who would not find such feelings frightening are men and women who are openly gay; but it may still be too big a risk to write about these feelings when there is still considerable homophobia in both the UK and the US.

So there are still areas of silence about the erotic transference and countertransference in therapeutic relationships. None the less there has been an enormous change in recent years. There is no longer such a danger-ous silence, the issues are discussed, a meaning is sought and therapists are less likely to feel frightened or guilty. Training courses are devoting some time to the therapeutic problems rather than ignoring them. The most important outcome is, or should be, a reduction both in the acting out of these feelings by a therapist and in the resultant sexual abuse of clients. This may be an explanation for the decreasing numbers of thera-pists who sexually abuse their clients.

The prelude to sexual abuse

Some years ago I attended a workshop on the maintenance of boundaries in therapy. The group of therapists was asked to list the small, and not so small, erosions of the boundaries that resulted in sexual abuse. Everyone in the group could list at least a dozen ways to erode the boundaries. Examples are over-familiarity, cracking dirty jokes, making suggestive remarks, having social meetings, touching, making the client special in some way, discussing the client's sex life or one's own sex life, insisting on secrets about counselling sessions, making the client a confidante for one's own problems. All of these can be a prelude to actual sexual advances, which range from commenting and touching in sexually suggestive ways, ogling or eyeing the client in a sexual way, asking the client to undress or undressing oneself, to dating and sexual contact including kissing, touching of breasts, thighs, bottoms and genitalia, oral sex and sexual intercourse, both genital and anal.

There has been some discussion in the professional associations on what constitutes a sexual act. Rutter (1990) suggests that 'any physical contact or bodily movement intended to express or arouse erotic interest is sexual behaviour'. This definition is particularly important when it comes to touch. Not all touch is sexual. Margaret Lyall (1997) makes a distinction between nurturing touch and erotic touch, and Smith (1998a) and Hunter and Struve (1998) both discuss the multiple meanings and functions of touch. The latter authors identify five positive uses of touch in therapy and identify nine main meanings and functions of touch, one of which is sexual. I will discuss touch and its use further in the next chapter. Currently the fear of being accused of sexual abuse is so great that often the advice given is never to touch a client. This is reinforced by the psychoanalytic tradition of no touch, which was discussed earlier in this chapter. Whilst this may be an over-reaction there are two other reasons for being cautious about touch. Firstly even if the intention of the touch is nurturing, a client, particularly one who has a history of sexual abuse, may misinterpret it, and secondly some of the research indicates that there is a relationship between touching patients and sexual contact. An example is the research of Holroyd and Brodsky (1980; cited by Garrett, 1994) who found that psychotherapists who had sex with their patients also advocated and used non-erotic touch with their patients more often than psychotherapists who had not had sex with any patients.

Pope, Sonne and Holroyd (1993) have produced as a result of their research a list of clues for therapists to warn them that they are approaching the slippery slope down which they could slide into sexual abuse. The warning clues for a therapist are finding oneself:

- dehumanising the client;
- dehumanising oneself;
- avoiding sessions e.g. cancelling sessions, arriving at the wrong time;
- obsessed with the client;
- making interesting slips and meaningful mistakes, e.g. dialling a client's phone number instead of a friend's;
- having fantasies of a client during sexual activities with one's sexual partner;
- giving a client undue special treatment;
- isolating a client;
- isolating oneself;
- creating a secret with a client;
- seeking repeated reassurance from colleagues;
- bored or drowsy in sessions.

Estelle Disch of Boston Associates to Stop Treatment Abuse has produced a very extensive checklist for therapists to alert them to possible boundary issues, which might interfere with their ability to work effectively with a client. It is reproduced as Table 3.1.

A number of associations set up to protect clients from abuse by therapists give lists of sexually abusive or exploitative behaviours. One such list is published by Survivors Against Abuse by Therapists:

With or without your consent, the counsellor:

- includes you in his/her social/family functions;
- borrows money or gets involved in business transactions with you;
- degrades, humiliates, intimidates or shames you;
- writes/sends love letters or encourages you to do so;
- dates you;
- makes sexual comments about your body;
- tells dirty jokes; shows pornographic material;
- talks about his/her sex life;
- touches you non-sexually in a way that makes you feel uncomfortable;
- encourages or demands sexual touch;
- removes clothing or asks you to remove clothing;
- says that being sexual or romantic with him/her is part of the counselling relationship;
- engages in sexual intercourse with you;
- ends the counselling relationship in order to become romantically or sexually involved with you.

It is equally important that clients are warned of the small steps that occur well before the client becomes aware of being sexually exploited. Russell (1993), as a result of interviewing clients who were sexually exploited by their therapists, found that before the sexual exploitation

TABLE 3.1 *Checking boundaries*

The purpose of this checklist is to alert you to boundary issues that might be interfering with your ability to work effectively with a particular client. Be particularly attentive if the situation persists even after you have attempted to change it.

1   This client feels more like a friend than a client.
2   I often tell my personal problems to this client.
3   I feel sexually aroused in response to this client.
4   I want to be friends with this client when therapy ends.
5   I'm waiting for therapy to end in order to be lovers with this client.
6   To be honest, I think the goodbye hugs last too long with this client.
7   Sessions often run overtime with this client.
8   I tend to accept gifts or favours from this client without examining why the gift was given and why at that particular time.
9   I have a barter arrangement with this client.
10   I have had sexual contact with this client.
11   I sometimes choose my clothing with this particular client in mind.
12   I have attended small professional or social events at which I knew this client would be present, without discussing it ahead of time.
13   This client often invites me to social events and I don't feel comfortable saying either yes or no.
14   This client sometimes sits on my lap.
15   Sometimes when I'm touching, holding or hugging this client during our regular treatment work, I feel like the contact is sexualised for one or the other or both of us.
16   There's something I like about being alone in the office with this client when no one else is around.
17   I lock the door when working with this client.
18   This client is very seductive and I often don't know how to handle it.
19   This client owes me/the agency a lot of money and I don't know what to do about it.
20   I have invited this client to public or social events.
21   I am often late for sessions with this particular client.
22   I find myself cajoling, teasing, joking a lot with this client.
23   I am in a heavy emotional crisis myself and I identify so much with this client's pain that I can hardly attend to the client.
24   I allow this client to comfort me.
25   I feel like this client and I are very much alike.
26   This client scares me.
27   This client's pain is so deep I can hardly stand it.
28   I enjoy feeling more powerful than this client.
29   Sometimes I feel like I'm in over my head with this client.
30   I often feel hooked or lost with this client and supervision on the case hasn't helped.
31   I often feel invaded or pushed by this client and have a difficult time standing my ground.
32   I sometimes hate this client.
33   I sometimes feel like punishing or controlling this client.
34   I feel overly protective toward this client.
35   I sometimes drink or take drugs with this client.

(Continued)

TABLE 3.1 *(Continued)*

36	I don't regularly check out what the physical contact I have with this client means for the client.
37	I accommodate to this client's schedule and then feel angry/manipulated.
38	This client's fee feels too high or too low.
39	This client has invested money in an enterprise of mine or vice versa.
40	I have hired this client to work for me.
41	This client has hired me to work for her/him.
42	I find myself talking a lot about this client with people close to me, even though they are not part of my supervision system.
43	I find myself saying a lot about myself with this client – telling stories, engaging in peer-like conversation.
44	If I were to list people in my caseload with whom I could envision myself in a sexual relationship, this client would be on the list.
45	I call this client a lot and go out of my way to meet with her/him in locations convenient to her/him.
46	This client has spent time at my home (apart from the office).
47	I'm doing so much on this client's behalf I feel exhausted.
48	I sometimes yell at this client.
49	I dread seeing this client.
50	I'm bored with this client and wish she or he would terminate.
51	I agreed to see this client for a very low fee and now I feel like I need to be paid more for my work but the client can't pay more.
52	I relate to this client in another role outside of the treatment relationship (e.g. student, research assistant, employee, family member, friend of a friend, etc.).

Source: Disch (1992) Reproduced by kind permission of Estelle Disch

started they almost always felt very special and dependent. Once the exploitation started they felt a betrayal of trust, as well as guilt, anger, frustration, helplessness, ambivalence and isolation, along with a poor or distorted self-image.

Such lists are valuable because they help educate the general public so they are better protected from the abusive therapist. It is lamentable that this is necessary but there is no way of discovering an exploitative therapist until after the sexual abuse has taken place. The general public has to be vigilant and knowledgeable so they know both what and what not to expect from a therapist who behaves and works ethically.

Strategies to prevent sexual exploitation

A dual relationship in which a client is sexually exploited is always harmful to a client, and the therapist who engages in such exploitation should not be allowed to practise. The problem is that none of the psychological therapies have statutory regulation. This means that associations such as BACP or UKCP can use as an ultimate sanction, permanent suspension from the association but this does not stop someone practising as a counsellor or psychotherapist. Until such time as the title is protected and no one may practise unless they are registered, the general public is very vulnerable. It is likely that within 10 years this will happen. Meanwhile the professions should be educating the public in what they should and should not expect. I know of no professional association that is doing this. In the UK this important task is being undertaken by POPAN. The associations do publish codes of ethics and practice or codes of conduct that expressly ban all sexual exploitation; but these codes are often long and complicated and do not give clients quick checklists. The professional associations need to do this and should be more helpful in other ways. Russell (1993) quotes a number of instances in which people she interviewed found the professional associations unhelpful.

People who have been sexually abused will almost certainly feel very uncertain about lodging a complaint, partly because two of the effects are self-doubt and low self-esteem. In addition they often feel as though they are betraying their therapist rather than doing the right thing. When an association insists that everything must be in writing, sends complicated codes, requires the client to select which of a number of clauses are relevant, and also has complicated procedures to follow, clients will feel daunted and may just give up. This leaves a therapist who should have been reported, reprimanded and punished, untouched and likely to sexually abuse someone else. POPAN was formed because too many people felt they could not lodge complaints and then go through the enquiry without support. This POPAN gives. Some professional associations have ethics committees that decide whether a complaint should be investigated. Russell (1993) reports that some clients found that the therapist who abused them was a member of the ethics committee, and so they believed that the professionals collude to protect each other. All professional associations should have a committee made up of executive staff of the association to handle the complaint initially and should use members of the association only on the adjudication panels. Obviously no professional member must know the therapist being accused of sexual exploitation or have a vested interest in the complaint being dismissed. It is good practice to ensure that at least one member of the panel is a lay-person. The professional associations must do everything in their power to remove any suspicion of collusion.

The professional associations also need to ensure that all training courses do look in detail at the likelihood of erotic transference and countertransference and give training in how to handle both. Until recently the topic was taboo and therefore left out of training programmes. To quote one of Russell's interviewees (1993): 'He opened up the sexual side of me then didn't know how to deal with it.' Whereas another of her interviewees, who had been abused by a previous therapist, was able to tell her new therapist this and make it clear that it must not happen again. The therapist made a very clear contract with her and she was able to tell him when she felt sexually aroused and discover that she felt like this when she wanted to be held. Gradually it emerged, when the therapist admitted to feeling an erotic countertransference in one session, that she had always used sex when she actually wanted affection. This pattern was broken because the sexual feelings were acknowledged, not acted upon, and thus came to be understood. All therapists need to work in this way, and not be frightened by sexual feelings. It is, of course, natural to have these feelings in some relationships. One sign of maturity is the ability to contain them and not act on them.

In recent years David Mann has been running workshops throughout the UK to ensure that many more therapists are at ease with the erotic transference and countertransference. In her book Russell (1993) outlines five exercises to raise awareness that client–counsellor or counsellor–client sexual attraction is possible and to look at the myths, values and prejudices that prevent therapists from thinking about how they would react and then respond to clients who stated they were aroused by them. Both these initiatives are evidence that the profession is beginning to be more open about the normality of sexual feelings on the part of both the clients and their therapists. Within this context it is then possible for therapists to work without being frightened, which means that the client is less frightened, and for the profession to gain much more understanding of the complicated dynamics at play. The combination of better training of therapists and more knowledgeable clients is essential in reducing the incidence of sexual exploitation. It is a dual relationship that should never happen.

4

Non-Sexual Dual Relationships: The Management of Gifts and Barter

The number of therapists who sexually exploit their clients is low, which would suggest that the majority of people know that such exploitation is both morally and ethically wrong and harms their clients. Many of the therapists who sexually abuse clients would also acknowledge that they should not have done so and that it did harm their clients. It therefore seems clear that this type of dual relationship should be avoided and it is harmful to the client. Indeed nowadays all professional associations prohibit sexual exploitation of clients and almost always expel a perpetrator from their association.

A non-sexual dual relationship that is harmful to or exploitative of the client is unacceptable. However, it is not as simple as it sounds because not all non-sexual dual relationships are harmful or exploitative and some are unavoidable. This means that there is far less agreement on what should be prohibited and what is left to therapists' professional judgement. For instance to my knowledge only one professional association, the American Counseling Association, mentions bartering in its ethical code, and none mentions gifts: yet both require a judgement on the part of the therapist, because dual relationships are formed if either transaction is undertaken. In addition the therapist's judgement will be coloured partly by the nature of the relationship: what is harmful in one relationship might be therapeutic in another. In one therapeutic relationship it may be appropriate to visit a client whilst s/he is in hospital but in another it certainly would not. The aim of this chapter is to explore such issues, present what has been written about non-sexual dual relationships, offer examples of dual relationships and explore where the limits should be set: in other words to find where the limits are. This is critical because some recent research Gabriel (2001) has found clear evidence that clients can be harmed in non-sexual dual relationships. When this happens they go through a similar 'see-sawing' of powerful and extreme emotions as people in a sexual dual relationship with their therapist.

The frame

Most therapists describe the limits as either the boundaries to the relationship or the therapeutic frame. It is the actual limits of this frame and therapist's attitude to the boundaries that will influence any decisions about changing the frame and entering into a dual relationship. The concept of a frame to the therapy was first mooted by Marion Milner in 1952 (cited by Gray, 1994). She used the metaphor of a frame chosen by an artist to contain a picture as analogous to the containment set by a therapist in setting the rules for therapy. Gray (1994) suggests that this framework of care has connections with what a good-enough parent provides for a child. The framework offers continuity and consistency, both essential requirements for healthy emotional development; it also gives a structure to a relationship, which may well be novel to the client and therefore somewhat mysterious (Lott, 1999). Equally important, the therapeutic frame offers a boundary that limits the therapist's power. This is essential when the power balance, particularly at the start of the therapy, is weighted so much in the therapist's favour.

Most therapists, regardless of theoretical orientation, would agree that this basic framework means that clients can rely on a given appointment time, which will rarely be changed, and that the therapist will be reliable and consistent. If there are fees these are set and clearly presented so clients know what to expect if they want to cancel or change an appointment. Clients of counsellors in voluntary agencies and organisations, who pay no fees, also need to understand how missed and cancelled appointments are handled; they should be aware of whether the number of sessions is rationed and how a missed session is dealt with. In some counselling agencies the missed session is considered to be one from the ration for allocation. Regardless of setting, clients also need to be clear about how their holidays and breaks from therapy will be handled and they should know well in advance, wherever possible, when the therapist will be on holiday or away. In addition the sessions will be held in a suitable and safe environment. In other words as far as possible clients should not be surprised, so that their anxiety and fear are contained. A considerable number of complaints to professional associations occur because this frame is either not set or not kept. Examples are: no contract, a sudden rise in fees, no notification of holidays, and a sudden ending with no arrangements to assist the client. Of course these boundaries also help to make the therapist feel safe. Therapists cannot offer a secure base unless they themselves are secure both emotionally and physically.

All these boundaries, which frame the therapeutic work, are derived from the psychoanalytic method developed by Freud. In fact Freud's analytic frame was not only about consistency and continuity but principally about abstinence. The idea of abstinence arose from his theory that the mind is organised around preordained instinctive drives which lead humans always to seek relationships with their parents and significant others for gratification of these drives. The internal conflict is always between the reflexive drive for pleasure and the reality of the social and physical environment that contains much disappointment and pain. Freud suggested that the hopes and dreads that anyone brings into a relationship, including the analytic relationship, are based on unconscious infantile sexual and aggressive fantasies. 'The hopes derive from infantile impulses for oral, anal and oedipal gratifications and triumphs. Dreads derive from fantasised punishment (particularly castration) for forbidden wishes' (Mitchell, 1993). The aim of the psychoanalyst is to arouse these desires and also make them conscious by not gratifying them. Once made conscious, they can be recognised and renounced.

The psychoanalytic method is therefore for the analyst not to gratify their patients because doing so prevents the analysands from being able to discover their infantile illusions and desires and transform them into rational understanding. In practice abstinence means the analyst has to maintain anonymity, as far as this is possible, and frustrate the analysand's desire to transcend or alter the analytic frame. Techniques like maintaining an expressionless face (the blank screen), sitting out of sight of the analysand and not answering questions driven by curiosity are all used to attain anonymity. Examples of how the analytic frame might be challenged by an analysand are asking for changed session times or extra sessions, or to borrow a book or a handkerchief. Of course analysts also will catch themselves thinking about breaking the frame by, for instance, offering a book or a sweater without being asked to do so. To act on these thoughts or the analysand's requests is not considered good practice by a classical psychoanalyst. The whole experience is deliberately deprivatory. Mitchell (1993) comments that this rule of abstinence is so strong in all analysts that they will have 'at least a twinge of uneasiness from their "classical superego" when doing anything that may be gratifying'. Whilst few counsellors are trained in the strict analytic tradition, they do have considerable dilemmas and self-doubt about when to gratify and when not. The training of psychodynamic counsellors is closest to the psychoanalytic tradition and therefore the taboo on gratification is greatest for them. In conflicts between person centred and psychodynamic counsellors a common criticism from the former group is that psychodynamic therapists are too rigid and unfeeling about clients' well-being. This is countered by psychodynamic counsellors who accuse person-centred counsellors of being too gratifying to their clients. The development in theory led particularly by the psychoanalyst Stephen Mitchell challenges the anxiety of psychodynamic therapists about gratification and brings the two groups closer to one another.

Mitchell in collaboration with Greenberg (Greenberg and Mitchell, 1983) began to question Freud's picture of the mental world people create within themselves to handle conflict and distress. They were also aware, as were other analysts such as Winnicott, Guntrip, Sullivan and Lomas, that the deprivatory way of working used by the traditional analyst did not help some people, who found the method unbearable and therefore unusable. Some people needed a more nurturing and responsive relationship to begin to be able to understand themselves and free themselves from their emotional problems. Sands (2000) writes eloquently about her experience of therapy with a deprivatory and then with a responsive therapist in *Falling for Therapy*. It is clear that she was not helped by the deprivatory therapist. Mitchell in collaboration with Greenberg developed the work of the British objects relations school, and of ego- and self-psychologists to suggest that it is actually the interaction with others that creates the patterns in the mind rather than the mind being prestructured and driven by the need to use people to gratify drives. In other words, their theory emphasises the primacy of relationship, whether with one's family of origin, one's family and friends or one's therapist.

This major shift in focus reconceptualises the fundamental task of psychoanalysis from Freud's concept that infantile longings needed to be exposed, mastered and renounced to a relational project in which the analysand's experience of self and sense of personal meaning needs to be reclaimed and revitalised. This in turn asks for a fundamental shift in the therapist's position from being an external, evaluating and neutral observer to being a co-partner in the struggles of clients to find their personal meaning and how it has been distorted. The therapist is, of course, a transference figure and this needs to be made conscious to the client but the therapist also needs to give their client recognition and an emotional relationship in which the therapist is unafraid to become involved in the same issues that entangle the client. This idea of a relational therapy has been developed for counsellors by Paul and Pelham (2000).

The idea of frustrating the client's desires for gratification, which are seen to be intrinsic to the client, comes directly from Freud's drive theory. If this theory is replaced by Mitchell's relational theory then the desires of the client to alter the therapeutic frame that arise in therapy can be seen to be of external origin. Any request by the client is as an attempt to enlist the therapist in either an 'old pathogenic interactional scenario or in a new therapeutically needed relational configuration' (Stern, 1994). These requests are for 'something-in-particular' from 'someone-in-particular' and are co-creations of the relationship between the therapist and client. The task for the therapist is not to decide whether to gratify or frustrate a wish, but to find a way to confirm and participate in the particular client's subjective experience and then gradually establish the therapist's own presence and perspective (Mitchell, 1993). The therapist is taking part in an experiment to see whether the client's solutions to their childhood longings are helpful and from this the client will discover whether this was what they really needed and wanted. A person cannot discover that a life-long wish is unsatisfying unless it has been gratified at least once. This responsiveness does not mean that a therapist does just what the client wants, because some requests would be damaging, nor should the therapist do something that is alien to him or herself. The request is handled respectfully and thoughtfully by the therapist, who then endeavours to give a response that matches the relationship created by the client and the therapist. The therapist is seeking the optimal response. If the request is for something that is alien to the therapist or that the therapist believes to be harmful to the client, then it must be considered respectfully and refused in such a way that the client does not feel shamed and retains sufficient self-respect to negotiate something else which is acceptable to both parties.

Many aspects of Mitchell's relational theory are closer to the practice of person-centred counsellors than to that of the classical psychoanalyst. The person-centred therapist would not have a standard response to a request from a client but would view it in terms of the real relationship existing between the client and themselves. Hence a request from one client might be a straightforward manifestation of their relationship, from another it might reflect the client's needs to share some of the control over the work and in a third it might even be a dimension of a self-defeating pattern in relationships. In the first two cases the experienced person-centred therapist might accede to the request but in the third example they would be more inclined to explore the issues involved. In all cases, like the psychodynamic practitioner the person-centred thera-pist would be unwilling to accede to dangerous requests.

The way in which requests by clients for a dual relationship is handled by a counsellor – whether the request is for a different method of payment, or is the form of an invitation to a wedding, or for a hug, or to counsel a friend – will be hugely influenced by the attitude of the coun-sellor to boundaries and gratification. Therapists from a strict analytic background would sincerely believe that gratification was damaging to their client and therefore attempt to interpret the request rather than comply. On the other hand those with a relational approach would want to understand the request in the context of the present relationship and past relationships and would probably comply, to discover the signifi-cance of the request. This would be with the aim of offering a reparative as well as a nurturing relationship. A further factor in handling such requests might also be the length and nature of the therapeutic relation-ship. It is possible that the response to a request to alter the boundary and create a dual relationship might be different if the therapeutic relation-ship had been for four sessions rather than a long-term one. It will be clear from this that at times it would be hard for two therapists from different modalities to agree whether an act was potentially harmful to the client, although obviously if the client produces incontrovertible evidence of harm there will be no disagreement. With the possibility of such differences in opinion it is essential that therapists can explain their acts from a theoretical point of view.

I have looked at boundaries in some detail because most decisions about the wisdom or otherwise of establishing a dual relationship that neither harms nor exploits a client, but might be positive and life-enhancing, will stem from the therapist's attitude to boundaries. This will be addressed in the rest of this chapter and the next four chapters.

Gifts

Gifts are normally seen as tangible objects but of course there are times when a smile, or a child's first words, or the sudden understanding of a problem is a gift. Gifts in a therapeutic relationship will be both tangible and intangible; throughout this section I am only considering tangible gifts, as these are the ones that usually challenge the bounds of the therapeutic relationship. A gift is defined in the dictionary as something given freely by one person to another (Longman, 1991) and is normally a token of friendship, appreciation or gratitude, but it can also be a bribe to try to manipulate the recipient. Of course a gift from a client to a therapist could be any one of these, but a therapist also has to consider whether a gift could be a way, possibly the only way available to a client at that time, to impart a message. Simultaneously it adds another level to the relationship, changing the nature of the therapeutic relationship from solely a professional one to a dual relationship, mixing personal and professional. The second relationship that arises will depend on the client's motivation. In a survey of the small amount of psychoanalytic literature on gifts Amos and Margison (1998) found that gifts functioned in seven ways:

- as a symbolic exchange;
- to 'bind' the therapist and patient;
- to act out something that cannot be discussed openly;
- to elicit a response;
- as a precursor to a boundary violation;
- as a workable aspect of transference;
- as a defence against the transference.

Whilst all of these are possible motivations it must also be remembered that gifts have a cultural significance as well as a gendered significance. In many of the Far Eastern cultures gifts are an essential part of good manners, which continues in the West (Sue and Zane, 1987). For instance for the Japanese every hospitable act must be acknowledged with a gift. If this is the case then from the client's perspective the giving of a present to a therapist who is welcoming and friendly would be right and the therapist would be rude to reject the gift. The rejection could cause offence to the person and even to their family. This, of course, can be the case within Western cultures and in certain families. There is also some evidence that in the West women are much more likely to give gifts than men. These gifts would simply be seen as women's expression of themselves. Such differences need to be borne in mind when thinking about gifts.

Most professionals are careful about gifts for the reasons cited in the *Code of Ethics and Professional Conduct for Occupational Therapists* (Association of Occupational Therapists, 2000). It states that they 'must not accept tokens such as favours, gifts or hospitality from clients or their families or commercial organisations when this might be construed as seeking to obtain preferential treatment'. Some companies manage their concerns about the vulnerability to abuse of people receiving a gift by either insisting that any gifts are handed in and then shared by the members of the practice or company, or putting a financial limit on the value of gifts that can be accepted. Recently the Department of Health suggested that the limit for medical practitioners should be £25 and any gift of a greater value should be declared.

Amos and Margison (1998) found in a survey of therapists in the UK that only 8 per cent of those surveyed had not received gifts from clients. The most common gifts were alcohol and flowers, followed by handmade, creative gifts such as paintings, photographs, crafts and home-grown plants, fruits and vegetables. Almost half of the gifts were accompanied by something written. This could be a poem, prose or a card, often with very personal messages. The most usual time for a gift was at the end of therapy (61 per cent). Other predictable times for gifts were after the client had been on holiday or at a traditional celebration such as Diwali, Christmas, Easter or Hanukah. They found that over 90 per cent of gifts were accepted, but many of those surveyed felt that receiving gifts was problematic, as was managing the multiple levels of communication in a gift.

Some of the therapists felt discomfort because they were uncertain whether they should accept a gift. Perhaps this is because so little has been written about gifts, and also because they are not mentioned in any of the professional codes. In addition, therapists from an analytic background may be uncertain about whether they should be totally abstinent. The dilemmas are:

- Should I treat this simply as normal social behaviour?
- Should I accept graciously?

- Should/must I refuse the gift; would this hurt or offend the client?
- Should I explore the timing and meaning of the gift and then decide whether to accept it or not?
- What is the meaning?
- Is a boundary being challenged?

Amos and Margison found that when a gift was given at the end of a therapeutic relationship the majority of therapists accepted it graciously with a simple acknowledgement. However, some people did comment that they felt robbed of their role of looking for any disguised communications (Spandler et al., 2000), particularly if a client handed them the gift as they left the room. It is questionable whether a comment on a hidden communication or an interpretation is appropriate at this point, because the process at the end of a therapeutic relationship is about enabling the client to cross the boundary into a new relationship with the therapist. Part of the task of the therapist is to reduce the imbalance of power and recognise the new social status of the client. They are now *not* a client and they are no longer someone with a problem needing a therapist. The giving of a present is a way of taking control and creating a balanced relationship. An interpretation at this point maintains the power differential between the two. Perhaps it should simply be accepted that some clients need to give a gift at this point. The small gift is a more personal way of saying thank you and marking the change(s) that have taken place. For some clients there is no payment at the point of delivery, because counselling is supplied by their GP, their employer or a voluntary agency; this may lead them to want to do something more personal. However, even in the private sector where there is payment, gifts are still common. Here again it may well be that the gift is much more personal than money and clients want to make such a gesture.

One of the paradoxes of therapy, particularly if it is long-term, is that it is both personal and professional. A professional person, who is a specialist in understanding human relationships, offers time and undivided attention so that the client can talk intimately about themselves; perhaps telling the therapist some secrets that only a very close friend knows, or maybe nobody else knows. This certainly can confuse clients and therapists. There is evidence of this from the complaints received by the professional associations. This potential confusion does make the handling of gifts difficult. Hence the dilemma of what to do when a client offers a gift, especially when it is not marking the end of the therapeutic relationship. Some clients can be so hurt by the refusal of a gift, or the feeling that the therapist is 'making a meal' of the gift, when as far as they are concerned the gift is simply part of normal social behaviour, that continuing in therapy is impossible. Yet from the therapist's point of view the 'language' of gifts is fascinating and carries hidden messages. These fall into four categories, several of which are often there simultaneously, and are:

- the nature of the gift as a metaphor;
- information about the client's feeling about themselves, perhaps as yet inexpressible in words;
- information about the client's feelings about the therapist, perhaps as yet inexpressible in words;
- information about relationships in the past (transference), perhaps as yet inexpressible in words.

This means that very skilful timing and wording are required if the therapist is to bring in the idea that the giving of a particular gift at a particular time might be highly significant. Sometimes it is better to accept the gift and explore its significance later when the client feels less threatened. At other times the client is secure enough to explore why they feel snubbed or why the therapist is making a lot of fuss about something that the client thinks is unimportant.

There are many complex messages hidden in a particular gift. A very obvious example of a metaphor is a dormant flower bulb that may symbolise the hidden potential of the client waiting to flower. At the same time, but perhaps less obvious, there may be a challenge about the therapist's capacity to look after something properly, because unless the bulb is watered and fed it will never flower. There may also be a message about the client's belief that s/he is forgotten between sessions by the therapist. The bulb is with the therapist every day, and is therefore a tangible reminder of the client.

The complex messages attached to gifts is discussed by Spandler et al. (2000). Food, such as sweets or cakes, was seen as feeding the therapist with good things. Therapists reported enjoying these gifts and often sharing them with their family. Whether that was the intention of the client is not mentioned. Food was thought to carry more significance if given by anorexic clients who would not allow themselves to enjoy such food. It appeared that anorexic clients might be asking the therapist to enjoy something that they could not. Therapists reported liking the hand-made or home-grown gifts and saw them as evidence of the client's growth and a reminder of the positive aspects of the therapy. However, therapists also reported having strong negative feelings as they were given some presents. This could be either because of the manner in which the gift was given or because the therapist had a strong internal feeling, as if the gift had a 'kick' attached.

Sometimes the metaphor of the gift was understood as evidence of the client's negative feelings about the therapist or the therapy. Examples given by therapists were a book about therapy, a healing crystal and a paper-knife. The therapist saw the book about therapy as a negative comment about her skill. The healing crystal was seen by the therapist to carry a negative comment about her inner resources but it might have been an unspoken message from the client about their belief that they were too much to handle without additional strength. The paper-knife was shaped like a double-edged sword, and in many ways was just that! It was a handsome gift but it also probably represented the client's murderous feelings towards the therapist. Therapy finished abruptly shortly after this gift. The therapist is quoted by Spandler et al. (2000) as saying 'I still have and use the paper-knife – it reminds me of my failure to contain the therapy'. Two gifts were mentioned which expressed clients' depression or suicidal feelings. These were 'nearly dead flowers' and a sculpture of a black, depressed figure sitting with its head buried in its hands.

Exercise 4.1: Gifts

Pick examples from the following list of gifts and see what messages these gifts might carry.

Vase	Brooch	Bottle of wine
Painting	Embroidery	Candlestick
Shawl	Bowl	Flowers
Theatre tickets	Fruit	Paperweight
Clock	Photograph	Soap and cosmetics
Shirt	Knitted doll	Notecards
Cookery book		

All the gifts mentioned so far are of a relatively low value and probably not worth more than £25. There are anecdotal stories of therapists being offered and sometimes accepting presents of a much greater value. Spandler et al. (2000) mention a video camera and unspecified gifts worth £100s or even £1,000s. They also mention a therapist being offered a flat. Whilst they do not indicate what the therapist did about this, the wording suggests the offer was refused. It would be wise to refuse such presents because to accept them does make one much more open to accusations of being exploitative. There are a few extremely unpleasant individuals who become vindictive towards their therapists and accuse them of malpractice even when there has been none.

Sometimes it is hard to find the metaphor attached to a gift and if one tries too hard it may seem somewhat contrived. Equally important is why a client needs to give a gift. Some of the hidden messages are mentioned earlier in this chapter. Other reasons are that the giving of a present may be intended to ensure love and attention. The client's experience may be that these have to be bought and are not an unconditional part of a relationship. Another reason for a gift is that a person may be unable to accept a present without giving something in return. Thus the feeling that the therapist has 'given' them time and attention means that something needs to be given in return. There is evidence that when people feel very impoverished their self-esteem grows when they can also 'do' or 'give' something to the helper. If this is the case, the rejection of such a present may cause particular hurt.

There were many therapists in Spandler et al.'s (2000) survey who felt that the process of gift giving and receiving was a positive experience: both because they felt pleased and gratified by the gift and because they felt able to use it in a way that expanded the client's understanding of themselves. This was equally true of gifts which were expressing negative feelings. This type of present giving was seen as healthy. However, not all gifts are benign in intent, nor is the present giving healthy. Some therapists felt that on occasions gifts were 'demanding', or came 'with strings attached', were seductive, or were meant to 'please' or 'placate' the therapist or 'buy her off'. The latter was understood as a manoeuvre to ward off perceived or feared feelings, in particular the therapist's anger. There is no reason why this use of gifts should not become material for the sessions. They are only examples of non-verbal communication. It only becomes unhealthy if the therapist does not understand the meaning and gets drawn into an unhealthy relationship with the client. Such an example would be to respond to a seductive gift with a sexual response.

The evidence collected by Spandler et al. (2000) suggests that the majority of therapists in their survey did accept presents and also endeavoured to make sense of the gift with the client. Almost all these therapists were from a psychodynamic background. These practitioners are always stereotyped as being more rigid about their boundaries. If this is true it is probably reasonable to assume that the majority of therapists do accept gifts, though not all would want to interpret their meaning. Obviously care must be taken because for a few very damaged individuals the intention is to seduce or hurt the therapist professionally. If the therapist is self-aware, honest with themselves about their feelings, takes their work to supervision and has a personal rule never to have a sexual relationship with a client, then the handling of gifts is a rich and rewarding area of work.

The assumption of this section has been that it is only the client who gives presents to the therapist, but this is untrue. There is a tradition for some therapists to give clients presents. I am unaware of any research on this but I know from my own practice and talking to other therapists that there are two reasons for this. One is to give a small token present of something from the therapy room that acts as a transitional object to help bridge gaps between sessions. These gaps may be caused by a holiday or illness, and for some clients there are times when they are very vulnerable and the gap of a week between sessions is unbearable without a tangible reminder of the therapist and the therapy room. I have used small polished pebbles, shells or dried flowers, all of which sit in bowls in my consulting room. Even with such small objects that have no monetary value it is important to be clear whether the object is a gift or should be returned. I usually introduce the idea that something from the room might be helpful and then encourage clients to decide whether they want to return the object, or bring it backwards and forwards from their home to the therapy sessions, or keep the object at their house. This type of 'experiment' helps clients understand more about themselves.

The other time that some therapists give a present is to mark the end of long-term therapy. Just as clients take an enormous amount of care in what they choose to give therapists to mark the end, so do therapists. Therapists I have known have spent considerable time in thinking about something that symbolises the work done and the journey taken by the client. It is given as a token of appreciation of the work done together and as a mark of the privilege the therapist has felt in being invited to journey in such a way with another human being. As with any gift between therapist and clients it is unnecessary, and yet a symbol may be the only language available to mark something of huge importance to both parties.

Whether it is a therapist or a client giving a gift it does cross boundaries and certainly introduces a dual relationship. But there is such richness in this language of gifts that I believe that provided the therapist is aware of the need for the therapy relationship to be non-exploitative and recognises that boundaries are being changed then the language of gifts is there to be explored creatively, not prohibited through fear.

Barter

There is some overlap between barter and gifts, in that gifts are sometimes proffered in the expectation that something will be returned. Initially this could be seen as a bribe but it becomes barter when freely negotiated between both parties. In this section I am looking at occasions when clients are not able to or do not want to pay for therapy with money and instead offer something in kind in exchange for therapy: thus barter. Most therapists I know in the private sector have experimented at least once in accepting 'something in kind' for therapy because they do not want therapy to be limited only to those who can afford it, and because the need of some people is particularly poignant. There are occasions when a reduced fee still does not enable someone to receive therapy, but barter makes it possible. However, there are often difficulties, as the following example illustrates.

Mary lives in a small village where the GP does not provide counselling. She is disabled and the buses to the nearest town are infrequent. She discovers that Jean, who lives in the village and is unknown to her, is a counsellor. Mary approaches Jean asking if she would consider counselling her, but she is retired and has a low income so could not afford to pay Jean any money. However, she would be able to pay in kind by baking a pie and a cake each week.

Jean considered this carefully and agreed. Some months later Jean began to feel very bored with the apple pie and jam sponge, which were delivered each week at a different time from therapy. She was reluctant to ask for a different pie and cake because it would introduce her preferences into the counselling and would be asking the client to please her. Gradually she resented the apple pie and cake more and more.

There are also difficulties for a client in paying in kind, as illustrated in the next example.

Susan approached a therapist, Katherine, who had been very highly recommended by a close friend. She was very short of money, having been unemployed for some time. She suggested to the therapist that she could clean her house weekly in exchange for therapy. They agreed to this arrangement and that Susan should do four hours of housework in exchange for one hour's therapy, since cleaners were paid less per hour than therapists. As time went by, Susan began to resent doing four hours' work in exchange for one hour of Katherine's time. She also thought Katherine and her family lived like slobs and she resented clearing up their mess.

These examples present some of the complications in accepting a service in lieu of money. In both instances a dual relationship is set up because the client has become a cook or a cleaner as well as a client, and the therapist is an employer. Other possibilities are being offered a painting or a piece of handcraft made by the client, or produce from a garden. In all these instances the same type of questions and difficulties arise. The first difficulty is: how does one equate one hour of therapy with any service such as cleaning, gardening, baking, painting and decorating, or creating a picture or a porcelain mug? Some people would suggest that one hour of a therapist's time should equate with one hour of anyone else's time. However, the reality is that therapists earn more an hour than gardeners or cleaners, but on the other hand some very successful painters and craftspeople could charge considerably more per hour, were a painting or craft to be costed on an hourly rate for its production.

A second problem is what to do if the proffered exchange is either of no interest initially or becomes boring. Had the counsellor, Jean, in the first example realised that the contract was unspecific about the type of pie and cake she could have pre-empted the problem by agreeing that there should be a variety of cakes and pies. But would it be better to negotiate for the cost of the ingredients, the fuel to cook the pie and cake and the client's time than to accept them? Should you refuse someone therapy on the grounds that you cannot find something that the client can offer that you want, or should you accept something in which you have no interest? How does one negotiate a change if a certain commodity is no longer of use or interest?

A third difficulty is how to handle a situation in which the work or goods are substandard. Does one ignore the problem or try to address it? Addressing it is never simple but will be particularly difficult in a therapy relationship in which acceptance and positive regard are essential components. In addition it brings in the therapist's own agenda rather than attending to the client's. However, ignoring it may be equally unsatisfactory. It could be that the client is performing poorly to provoke a conflict.

There are similarities between the possible hidden language of gifts and barter. There may be significance in the choice of what is offered for barter and how it is delivered. Is the choice of food a means of feeding the therapist, because the client feels that the therapist is 'empty' and not giving enough? Is there a difference in meaning between the object of barter being brought to the session or left on the doorstep some days after the session? All of this will be a rich seam to explore.

I have outlined many of the difficulties in agreeing to accept something other than money in lieu of fees. Yet I know of people who have accepted barter and the arrangement has been satisfactory. The reason why there was no problem is that the therapist had thought about how to handle the request for barter and was aware of the difficulties that could arise. This meant they could be openly discussed in advance. It is also important that the client and therapist have a relationship in which difficulties for both parties can be discussed easily when they arise. The following is an example of a barter that worked well.

Nine months after Jack's partner died he found that he was still crying uncontrollably at some point on most days. He also found himself frequently picking up Peter's old sweater and hugging it for comfort. He began to worry that he was going mad. Friends tried to reassure him but when this failed they suggested to him that he might find it helpful if he talked to a therapist. Jack wanted to do this but he earned very little money and felt embarrassed about asking for help when he knew he couldn't pay.

He went to see a therapist, Helen, and explained his dilemma. She felt very concerned about him and suggested that six sessions would be enough for him to understand and accept his feelings. Peter mentioned that he had very little money, but wondered if Helen would accept one of his pots in lieu of fees. She suddenly realised why she knew his name. It was because she had seen his pots in a local craft shop and had admired them. Helen had accepted barter before so she was aware that it could be difficult. With this in mind she said to Peter that in principle she was happy to exchange a pot for therapy but they would have to work out an agreement that they were both happy with. The most important thing was that they both accepted the deal and neither felt cheated. Peter already knew her fee and suggested that he should 'pay' for his sessions with two pots, which Helen felt was fine. They also explored whether Peter should choose the pots for Helen or vice versa. They agreed that at the last session he would bring six of his pots and Helen would choose which two she would like. They both felt happy with this arrangement and the therapy went well.

Most of the problems that arise with barter can also occur when a client belongs to a Local Exchange and Transfer System (LETS). In 1996 about 1,000 places in the English-speaking world had such systems (Douthwaite, 1996). These systems have been set up by local communities and do not use money but instead have special cheques denominated in the local unit. In Bradford the local unit is Brads, in the Beara peninsula of Eire it is Hags. When someone joins the scheme they are issued with a chequebook and a directory of services and goods wanted and on offer. As with any trade, the two parties decide how much each job or commodity is worth and then the cheque is lodged with the system's accountant. Members of the system receive statements regularly. If therapists are not part of this system they have to decide whether they wish to join. Joining would involve negotiating with clients what an hour of therapy is worth in the local LETS unit and discussing the wisdom or otherwise of a direct exchange of services. I would advise against a direct exchange of therapy for a service, because of the complexity of the additional relationship. Although a LETS system removes some of the difficulty of a straight barter for goods or services it is still complex in terms of the value of the service.

The American Counseling Association discourages bartering 'because such arrangements create inherent potential for conflicts, exploitation and distortion of the professional relationship' (ACA, 1997). However, it does not prohibit it: instead it states that 'counsellors may participate – only if the relationship is not exploitative, if the client requests it, if a clear written contract is established, and if such arrangements are accepted practice among professionals in the community'. This seems very good advice. I would add that any therapist contemplating agreeing to barter should both be very clear about the difficulties and warn the client of these but also be aware that even if a barter is agreed freely at the start of the relationship feelings might change. Therapists need to be on the lookout for changes in feeling in themselves as well as in their clients and make certain these difficulties are recognised and worked with and not left to fester. If they are left to fester that is when dissatisfaction can arise and may result in the client making a complaint to the professional association.

5

Touch: Finding the Limits

I have included touch in this book because the introduction of touch into a therapy session crosses one of the boundaries set and alters the dynamics of the relationship. This may give the therapist an additional role of physical caregiver, and may bring up the question of friendship during and after therapy. The introduction of friendship during therapy definitely creates a dual relationship. It is less clear whether touch alone initiates a dual relationship. In this section the question is whether touch can be used safely, ethically and effectively.

Fear of touch

Touch was mentioned in the third chapter because it is so often a prelude to sexual exploitation of a client by a therapist. Therapists appear to have responded to those unethical practitioners who sexually abused their clients by making touch a taboo, rather than condemning the practitioners. However, Wilson (1982; cited by Hunter and Struve, 1998) suggests that 'the touch taboo is not deterring many therapists from using touch, but is strong enough to keep them from admitting it to one another'. Recent research by Tune (2001) confirms this. In his small sample of six British therapists from five different theoretical orientations 15 examples of touch were mentioned by the therapists, initiated by the therapists in nine cases. At first all but one answered 'no' to the question of whether they touched their clients; Tune concluded that they were ambivalent about discussing this either with him or with their supervisors. From this it would appear that for some, perhaps for many, there is a theoretical rather than a practical touch taboo, which has resulted in people being frightened to admit publicly that they touch their clients and also fearful about writing about it or doing research in this area. It is interesting in this context that in 1998 two books were published on touch in psychotherapy; *Touch in Psychotherapy* edited by Smith, Clance and Imes and *The Ethical Use of Touch in Psychotherapy* by Hunter and Struve. I will quote quite extensively from both, because although there is some overlap they more often complement one another.

Smith (1998b) comments on the oddity of the taboo on touch within therapy when touch in healing, for instance the laying on of hands, has very ancient roots and is still used today. Many alternative therapies, such as aromatherapy and reflexology, and therapies complementary to medicine, such as chiropractic, osteopathy and massage, use touch extensively; and in orthodox medicine health care workers, such as physiotherapists, frequently use touch in diagnosis and treatment. In the early days of psychiatry most interventions were physical, so it is unsurprising to find that Freud used touch in the early days of psychoanalysis, and suggested that 'the ego is ultimately derived from bodily sensations', with the implication that the lack of bodily sensations, would limit ego-development (Freud, 1923; cited by Hunter and Struve, 1998). Later he dropped all use of touch as he developed his drive theories and, as mentioned earlier, came to believe that touch, which would only be done to gratify a patient's need, would interfere with the transference. Thus in psychoanalysis touch is taboo. However some of his followers, for example Ferenczi and Reich, disagreed: most of the modern day body-oriented psychotherapies, such as bioenergetics and biodynamic psychotherapy, were developed from Reich's work and the use of touch 'is an integral part of the theory and technique' (Tune, 2001). There is also evidence that humanistic therapists touch their clients 25 per cent more than psychodynamic practitioners (Holroyd and Brodsky, 1980; cited by Tune, 2001).

Research on touch

The three obvious areas for research on the use of touch in therapy are: whether there are negative effects of touch, whether lack of touch could be or is damaging, and whether there are positive effects of touch. In fact the research evidence is fairly sparse. Research on the negative effects of touch has mainly been concerned with touch leading to sexual abuse, which was discussed in an earlier chapter. However there are two other pieces of research on the negative effect of touch. Sussman and Rosenfeld (1978; cited by Hunter and Struve, 1998) found that touch given without permission as opposed to anticipated touch was perceived negatively. Geib (1982; cited by Hunter and Struve, 1998) in a study of the responses to non-erotic touch of 10 women clients in therapy with men found that for four women it was detrimental because:

- they felt 'trapped in the gratification of being close';
- they felt guilty towards the therapist whom they perceived as nurturing;
- they felt responsible for the therapist's well-being; thus there was a role reversal;
- the relationship with the therapist was a recapitulation of their childhood family dynamics.

There were people in the survey who found the experience of non-erotic touch positive, which will be mentioned shortly. The negative effects could be taken as very strong reasons why touch should not be used in therapy, and they certainly indicate the pitfalls to be expected if one decides that touch is an appropriate therapeutic activity. The counter-argument is that therapists who use touch therapeutically must expect a variety of responses, including negative responses to touch. The therapist should explore the responses and reactions to touch and any misperceptions become material from which to understand more about the client and their emotional world; like all unexpected and unusual responses, they become grist to the mill.

There seems to be no literature about the effects of lack of touch in therapy but there are personal accounts. Many therapists with a strict analytical training do not shake hands with clients on arrival or parting. Yet as France (1988) comments, writing about the experience of being a client, 'it is not uncommon for bank managers, solicitors or other sorts of medical consultants to shake hands. The gesture itself simply means "We are meeting or parting on good terms, as equals" so it would not be inappropriate in psychotherapy.' Dinnage (1989), also writing from a client's perspective, mentions the need for 'normal friendliness' and Sands (2000), again from this viewpoint, questions why analysts should think it pertinent to explore a client's feelings of discomfort in response to their 'ungracious behaviour' of not shaking hands and greeting them with a 'stony silence'. Sands asserts that it would be normal to be discomforted by such strange behaviour, which bears 'little resemblance to the way human beings usually treat each other'. Clients are bound to be puzzled and possibly upset unless they are led to expect such behaviour and are given some explanation of its purpose. Even with an explanation such as that the therapist is testing whether one can bear a deprivatory relationship, it will certainly drive some people away, create a challenge for others and slow down the formation of a working alliance for yet others (Lomas, 1987). In normal life withholding of touch generally gives an unpleasant feeling of distance and conveys hostility or anger. This lack of warmth was one of a number of reasons why Anna Sands was unhappy with her first therapist. Ann France (1988) particularly mentions touch and her own experience of three therapists. The first and third ones did not touch her at all; the middle one did touch her and subsequently withdrew touch. She comments of the first therapist:

> I remember thinking wistfully sometimes that it would be comforting if she were to put her arms round me when I was miserable, but the years went by and she never did. I got used to that as part of the frustrating experience inherent in therapy, exactly as I had seen as a child how other people's parents hugged

them or comforted them and mine never did. As far as the psychotherapy went, I don't think it did me any harm, though there is no way of knowing how much the occasional gesture of warmth might have been more therapeutic.

It might have encouraged greater dependence, but, in the same way good mothering encourages healthy emotional growth, it might have given me a sense of being less repulsive and more acceptable. It seemed to me at the time that there was emotional dependence without gratification. I didn't become more capable of mothering myself or of receiving or giving affection. (France, 1988: 194–195)

As Ann France herself says soon after this passage, 'there is no direct control' to establish whether the therapy would have been more effective and/or have taken less time if there had been physical holding. However, therapists should accept feedback from their clients and at least challenge themselves about whether the absence of physical touch could be detrimental and whether there is a place for physical holding as well as the Winnicottian metaphorical or moral holding.

Interestingly, although the introduction of the word 'holding' by Winnicott was a metaphor to describe a safe and well boundaried therapeutic environment in which no touch took place, he did touch some patients. Margaret Little (1985), who was in analysis with Winnicott and an analyst in her own right, describes how he held her hand during sessions, which she believed fostered her psychological growth. This personal account of the positive effects of touch is supported by the research of Horton, Clance and Sterk-Elifson (1995; cited by Hunter and Struve, 1998). They found that 69 per cent of the respondents in a sample of 231 clients said that 'touch fostered a stronger bond, facilitated deeper trust, and contributed to greater openness with the therapist' and 47 per cent said that the use of touch enhanced their self-esteem. This publication is one of the few studies on the positive effects of touch. A number of other studies with positive effects are suspect because the participants were fellow students of those doing the study, which may introduce a bias (Hunter and Struve, 1998). As with the effects of lack of touch, much of the information about the positive effects of touch is anecdotal and comes from clients who have had therapists who touched them. Ann France's second therapist did put 'a pair of warm steady hands' on her shoulders as she cried. This was unexpected, partly because she knew the rules that forbade touching and also she had not been touched by her first therapist. France (1988) reports that she continued to cry but felt more secure and less terrified and lonely. Subsequently she did not know whether it would happen again but found the memory gave her a feeling of worth and enabled her to manage a period of separation from the therapist and make some good new relationships. In fact the gesture was repeated at rare intervals and each time she found that feelings of inner worth were engendered which lasted over the next separation. Problems arose when following another separation France became depressed for two years, during which time her therapist made no physical contact. During this time she was obsessed by the need for physical contact of some sort whereas when touch was available 'the wish [to be touched] did not have to be gratified often, as long as it sometimes might be'. She never mentioned this increasing obsession to her therapist nor questioned why physical contact had ceased, but assumed that withdrawal was either a deliberate policy or a 'mere lack of inclination'. Neither explanation was satisfactory because one was 'too theoretical' and the other confirmed her self-hate.

When preparing her book France did give the therapist who had withdrawn contact an opportunity to comment on her actions, and she included her comments in her book. The therapist's reasons for withdrawing were that she feared that she 'was dragging [Ann France] into a dependence which might become too much'; and she also felt in the countertransference that Ann France was trying to rid herself of dependence. This latter observation is important because it illustrates the dilemmas for a therapist about whether her countertransference feelings are projections from the client or her own fears about dependency. This type of dilemma is common and is one reason why supervision of all therapeutic work is essential, but particularly so if one is offering something that one begins to feel is not helpful to the client.

This experience of Ann France is also interesting because it illustrates what happens when therapists change their behaviour without explanation, whether it is introducing touch or withdrawing it. The necessity for clients to feel involved in any decisions about physical contact is clear from the research of Geib (1982; cited by Hunter and Struve, 1998: 106) who found that five requirements were essential if non-erotic touch were to give a positive outcome. These were:

- the patient [sic] and therapist discussed the 'touch event', the boundaries of the relationship, and the actual or potential sexual feelings;
- the patient felt in control of initiating and sustaining contact;
- contact was not experienced as a demand or need for the satisfaction of the therapist;
- the overall expectations of the treatment [sic] were congruent with the patient's experience of the treatment;
- the emotional and physical intimacy were congruent.

A small number of psychotherapists and psychoanalysts have written about the need for touch with particular clients and at particular times, giving theoretical reasons for this and also examples from their own work (Prodgers, 1986; Woodmansey, 1988). These authors differ from Winnicott because he only advocated actual physical holding for patients with very deep disturbances who were in psychoanalysis and being seen five times a week, whereas they are suggesting that physical contact can be appropriate for psychotherapy and counselling clients. They are all clear that for certain people physical contact during therapy is helpful and therefore it should be provided, and for others it is not only unhelpful but also harmful and should not be offered. Thus there is a place for both a nurturing type of therapy and for a more deprivatory one. Both modes of therapy are offering corrective experiences. For some people the correction is intended to replace a deficit of warmth, touch and holding, which is a proper part of good parenting, with reparenting. This may need to include touch, particularly if the deprivation was preverbal, because verbal explanations are of little use in repairing the deprivation when it was early feelings of well-being that were absent, not words. For healing to take place these feelings of worth arising from being touched and held are internalised and a deficit replaced.

Many therapists believe that the reparation of the lack of physical contact as an infant by concrete touch is insufficient and that words have also to be found to turn the deficit into a psychic concept so the client can gradually give to herself the comfort initially coming from the therapist. An example of this is given by Rosenberg (1995). She was first trained as a bioenergetics therapist and subsequently trained as a psychoanalytic psychotherapist. A consequence of this was that one client remained with her through the transition from one way of working to another. Rosenberg believes that her work with the client would have run into an impasse had she not embarked on a psychoanalytic training, which meant that the physical touching ceased and was replaced by interpretation of the 'transferential meaning of what was happening' so that the client 'acquired the psychic capacity to put her feelings into words'. In this therapy the touching was followed by interpretation because of the therapist's change in orientation. More usually where the therapist remains in one theoretical orientation the two would be integrated and timed to meet the client's needs as the client moved from regressed to adult states. A second way in which the use of touch can offer a corrective experience is for those clients for whom touch has always been abusive. A new language about touch has to be learnt and this may only be possible using touch. It should be clear that a considerable number of therapists believe that there are therapeutic reasons for contact and expressions of ordinary warmth and as with any other therapeutic intervention it has to be thought about, discussed in supervision and then an active decision made to use it or not.

Before using touch safely and therefore ethically a therapist must have training. The areas that need to be explored are power dynamics; the effect of culture, ethnicity and gender on the interpretation of touch; the multiple meanings and functions of touch; and the clinical uses of touch.

Power dynamics

The understanding of the part that power dynamics play in the use of touch is particularly important because so many clients have been the victims of abuse by powerful people and frequently part of the abuse involves misuse of touch. The power dynamics are affected by people's status, cultural/ethnic background and gender. These factors also can affect how touch is interpreted (Hunter and Struve, 1998).

In general there are rules in Western cultures which give permission to the superior-status person to touch the inferior-status person and it is considered an act of defiance if touch is initiated by the latter (Henley, 1973; cited by Hunter and Struve, 1998). It must be remembered that touch increases intimacy and therefore vulnerability in clients who are already vulnerable. It is critical not only that therapists check that they are using their power positively but also that the touching is being used to promote mutuality rather than domination. The cultural or ethnic background of clients must also be understood; there are enormous differences between racial and cultural groups in their use of touch. For example Latin Americans and Mediterraneans (including Jewish and Arabic societies) and some African societies have a greater frequency of touch compared with Americans, Germans and English, who come from non-contact cultures. Within the United States, Californians seem to touch each other more than New Englanders, and in the so-called non-contact countries the physical embrace between two football players is acceptable. There are also gender differences in response to touch, although it is difficult to be definitive about this because the results of research is conflicting, probably because the issues of status and sociali-sation confuse the picture. In both the American and British cultures men are commonly socialised to sexualise intimacy, so touch which increases intimacy can easily be misinterpreted, whatever the intention of the toucher.

Hunter and Struve (1998) suggest that in considering the use of touch therapists have also to be aware of the great variety there is in the sub-jective experience of being touched. Both the physiology and psychology of different individuals affects this. An example of a physiological difference is where the sensory perception of what occurred could be different from what the toucher did; thus a soft pat could be perceived as excruciatingly painful. This may be because the sensory end-organs are over-sensitive. A psychological difference can be seen where for some individuals a soft touch on the arm that is intended to be comforting is perceived as conde-scending. This misreading is likely to be linked to earlier experiences of touch. Touch is often linked to either violence or sexual abuse and there-fore the victims will make incorrect associations. This is a good example of where some therapists would feel it a valid therapeutic endeavour to encourage the formation of correct associations in which touch is associated with nurturing and comfort rather than violence or seen as a prelude to sexual abuse.

Hunter and Struve highlight two further factors which they suggest must be understood by any practitioner contemplating using touch therapeutically. These are that unexpected touch can be disturbing, and that there are social and cultural rules about bodily contact and personal space. An obvious example is that when people in Britain can choose their seating in an auditorium they will leave an empty seat between themselves and a stranger and will only sit next to them if the hall is very full. In addition people have vastly different tolerance of and comfort with intentional and accidental touch.

Smith (1998a) adds a further important point about touch, which is that it is often emotionally more powerful than words. It is both powerful and risky because therapists who use touch make their presence felt more strongly and their interventions are likely to be more forceful.

Meanings and functions of touch

There is a tendency to consider touch as 'a homogeneous, unidimensional phenomenon' (Smith, 1998a) but in fact it is has multiple meanings and functions. Every therapist who uses touch therapeutically, and therefore also has to decide when not to use touch, must be aware of the complexity of the language of touch. Hunter and Struve (1998) list the following functional categories:

- accidental touch such as when someone brushes against someone else;
- task-oriented touch which may be intentional such as steadying someone to prevent them falling, or unintentional when money is exchanged;
- attentional touch to gain or hold someone's attention. Other forms are: (a) touch for greeting or departure; (b) referential touch which is used to draw attention to a part of the body and (c) courtesy touch linked to a ritual;
- celebratory touch, often a spontaneous response of joy, excitement or pride in response to someone's achievement;
- affectional touch, an expression of friendly, helpful or playful emotional energy;
- emotional touch, which accompanies the expression of an emotion; and an emotion may be expressed only by touch. Emotional or expressive touch may be used to convey appreciation, to reinforce a

response (smacking reinforces displeasure whereas a hug has the opposite purpose), to support, nurture, reassure or protect, to indicate affection or sympathy, to be playful or to induce catharsis and release emotions that may be being held back;

- sensual touch, which can have sexual overtones, but can simply be intended to gratify the senses and be soothing, as happens when two friends or relations touch and caress each other tenderly;
- aggressive touch expressing agitation, disapproval, anger or rage;
- sexual touch, which is physical contact with overt or implicit erotic overtones (see Chapters 2 and 3).

All but the first two and last three categories on this list could deliberately be used by a therapist if touch is a conscious and chosen tool. Sexual touch should never happen in a therapeutic relationship and nor should sensual touch because it is too open to confusion with sexual touch. A therapist must never attack or provoke a client to attack them; provoking aggression in a client could be a way of expressing one's hostility to the client and acting it out in so-called self-defence. However if a therapist is attacked then it is reasonable that he or she should defend himself or herself 'using only the force necessary to neutralise the attack' (Smith, 1998a). It is not acceptable for the therapist to be aggressive in self-defence.

Obviously accidental touch can occur in a therapeutic relationship. An example would be when either the client or therapist uncrosses their legs and brushes against or knocks the other. Many would see this as accidental and simply clumsy in a non-therapeutic relationship, but within the therapeutic relationship, particularly for a psychodynamic practitioner, an important question is whether it has a hidden, unconscious meaning. It could be an expression of hostility, or a prelude to sexual advances. It is also possible that the knock was intentional but disguised as unintentional. Hunter and Struve (1998) suggest that the therapist must acknowledge the contact verbally with an apology or indication of a mistake because clients who have been sexually abused may interpret such touch as a prelude to abuse. Regardless of a therapist's theoretical orientation a therapist has be alert to the possibility of hidden meanings and reactions to any accidental act, however brief, that occurs in therapy. It is equally important that the client's reaction to the therapist's accidental act is explored and that therapists check with themselves and possibly with their supervisors that the apparently accidental act was indeed just that. This is also true of a task-oriented touch when again touching can occur which appears accidental, for example touching or knocking the therapist as payment is made.

Attentional touch can be used to focus attention or control behaviour. In therapy gently touching a client who has severely regressed or is in a trance may help them return to the present and reground them. Other forms of attentional touch also occur in therapy. A handshake on greeting someone is common socially and is therefore offered by some clients on first meeting a therapist. This normal act may reduce a person's anxiety. The rejection or questioning of this by a therapist may make the client so uncomfortable that it is perhaps unwise to do so at the very beginning. In my experience few clients offer a handshake after the first session and a verbal greeting is most common. On more than one occasion male clients have persisted in shaking hands with me. This has always given me an uneasy feeling and a 'shiver down my spine', which I have examined in supervision to check whether it is a response because of personal issues or a significant countertransference response. On most occasions it has been the latter and has been a sign that the male client has a vicarious sexual relationship with me. Some clients have been very defensive when I have explored this with them but have gradually been able to acknowledge that the handshake had sexual overtones for them. A handshake at the end of a meeting is also a social norm, particularly for men; as with the greeting handshake, it is rarely offered after the first session. Again if it persists it will be important both to check one's feeling about it and to explore it with the client. Some clients do ask for a hug at the beginning or end of a session and a lot of clients ask for one verbally or initiate one at the end of the last session. If it is part of one's normal therapeutic behaviour to hug someone on request it is important also to establish the meaning of the hug and the reason for it. Some clients only need it during a phase in therapy in which they feel very young or insecure, or both, and later have no need for a hug. It is equally important to explore the significance of ending hugging. At no time should it be assumed that the hug or brief contact should become a precedent.

Another type of attentional touch used in therapy is the referential touch. An example of this is where a client feels ashamed about a scar, disfigurement or a part of their body and may ask a therapist to look at or touch that part of the body. An example might be a client who is living alone, has few close friends and is very ashamed of and embarrassed by her disfigured stump following an amputation. She might ask a therapist to look at her stump and touch it gently. This could be very healing if it counters the client's belief that no one can bear to look at or touch her stump because it is so ugly. Up to that point the only other people to have seen her stump may have been medical personnel whose task is to check it as part of a routine job rather than to recognise the person's pain and shame about the disfigurement.

Within the overall category of attentional touch Hunter and Struve (1998) also identify courtesy touch. Obviously touch for greeting and departing is one type of courtesy touch. In therapeutic relationships a courtesy touch might also be part of a ritual such as holding hands during a closing circle at an experiential workshop.

Celebratory and affectional touch are placed in one category by Hunter and Struve (1998) perhaps because both tend to be spontaneous and arise out of the emotional connectedness between two people. In any long-term therapy this is likely to exist. The celebratory touch would occur in response to good news, which is as likely to happen to a person within a therapeutic relationship as anywhere else. If a therapist has made a conscious decision not to use touch then s/he is likely to have to actively suppress her/his celebratory response because it is so spontaneous. This is likely to be true of the affectional touch as well. If affectional touch is used to offer nurture, encouragement, caring, comforting or reassurance then it should only be used by an experienced therapist in a 'solid psychotherapy relationship' (Hunter and Struve, 1998) and never without a verbal explanation of the intended meaning. This is because it is so open to misinterpretation by the client, with context, timing and the nature of the therapeutic relationship affecting how it is translated. It is also vital that the therapist monitors very carefully the client's response and any subsequent changes in behaviour that would indicate how the affectional touch has been received.

There are close similarities between some aspects of emotional or expressive touch and affectional touch in that they are open to misinterpretation and therefore need clarification and the client's response must both be monitored and worked with. Again they should only be used in a solid long-term therapy and it is unwise for an inexperienced therapist to use them. It should only be the client that initiates appreciative touch. Therapists should be mature and self-aware enough to know when they are appreciated and they should not need to initiate acts of gratitude. Touch may be used to reinforce a response and might therefore be used in cognitive behavioural therapy and in aversion therapies and could be closely related to cathartic touch. In the latter, emotions are sometimes identified as being focused in a particular part of the body; touching that area of the body may release the trapped emotion. This is done by body therapists. Touch can express nurture, support and care and therefore overlaps with affectional touch. For many clients and therapists a major role of therapy is support, so deciding whether this type of touch is appropriate and likely to be helpful to the client is going to be common. Hunter and Struve (1998) suggest that this type of touch will involve using the hands or a gesture rather than a hug. Ann France's experience of 'a pair of warm, steady hands' on her shoulders, which was mentioned earlier, is an example of this. Often a gentle touch is the most helpful thing one can do with a deeply grieving client. Colin Murray Parkes (2001) in describing helping the bereaved in New York following the destruction of the World Trade Center Towers on September 11, 2001 states that 'You touch the bereaved, put your arm round them. As a psychiatrist I was always told that you should never touch your patients because it is a kind of sexual seduction, but at times like this you have got to touch people. It's the most natural thing to do. It has an immediate effect.' This type of touch is probably both supportive and protective when someone is experiencing emotions that are searing. The touch conveys the presence of another human being who is there with you and feeling with you. Another type of protective touch may occur in a therapeutic relationship if it is necessary to touch someone to prevent self-harm or an accident. It is unlikely that a playful affectionate touch will be used between a therapist and client but it might be used in group therapy between two facilitators. One therapist might realise that the other is over-reacting to something or is too intense and might model a way of defusing it by gently kicking his co-therapist's shin, while smiling.

There is considerable overlap in the function and meaning of touch, as can be seen from the examples given above of the different functions that touch may have when it is used in therapy. These have been summarised by Hunter and Struve (1998: 127–35) as:

- to reorient a client;
- to emphasise a point;
- to access memories or emotions;
- to communicate empathy;
- to provide safety or to calm a client;
- to assist in enhancing confidence and self-worth;
- to change the level of intimacy;
- as an adjunct to hypnosis;
- to assist in the resolution of stuck emotions arising from childhood abuse or trauma.

This list overlaps with one drawn up by Lyall (1997: 28–30) when writing about her use of touch as a pastoral counsellor. She identifies five types of touch that might be appropriate at particular times. These are:

- as a ritual in the social sense, e.g. a touch on entering or leaving;
- in crisis situation, e.g. grief, trauma, depression or other acute illness, to ground the client and provide reassurance that they are not alone in the crisis;
- to focus the client's attention if wandering;
- to emphasise a verbal statement;
- to unblock a client.

Lyall also gives useful indications of when not to touch a client. These are:

- when the therapist does not want to touch for whatever reason;
- when the client does not want to be touched;
- when touch would encourage the client to avoid the therapeutic process altogether by being content with infantile gratification;

- when the client has not reached the depths of their pain and touch could block further progress;
- when the therapist feels manipulated by the patient;
- when the therapist is aware of the temptation to manipulate the client;
- when touch involves the counsellor colluding with the client because their own pain is triggered. (1997: 31–3)

Clinical functions of touch

Hunter and Struve (1998) have reclassified the types of touch that occur in therapeutic relationships into five clinical functions. These are:

- providing real or symbolic contact;
- providing nurturance;
- facilitating access to, exploration of and resolution of emotional experiences;
- providing containment;
- restoring touch as a significant and healthy dimension in relationships.

The decision of whether to offer touch or not will depend on both theoretical and ethical considerations. Orthodox psychoanalysts do not touch their clients for theoretical reasons, though there is little research to support this. The relational theory of some psychotherapists supports the use of touch in certain instances, as do most regressive and some humanistic theories. Here again there is little research but some of the research and some subjective accounts of clients do suggest that there are positive effects of touch. It is also clear that non-erotic touch can have negative effects. The ethical considerations are firstly whether the therapist has adequate training both theoretically and technically in the use of touch. Secondly therapists must not use touch if it is any way alien to themselves. Thirdly touch should be offered only if it is really in the service of the client's needs.

If a therapist is convinced that both theoretically and ethically the use of touch is acceptable then s/he must proceed with caution. The therapist must know enough about a client's history to have a map in their mind of which zones of the client's body are erogenous zones and which areas when touched will rekindle memories of sexual or physical abuse. These areas should not be touched initially and a client's erogenous zones must never be touched. The research by Geib (1982; cited by Hunter and Struve, 1998) quoted earlier gives clear guidelines as to the environment a therapist must create for touch to be used safely. The client must be in control and agree to the use of touch. The timing of its introduction is crucial because it must be paced so it is congruent with both the physical and emotional intimacy of the therapeutic relationship. There must be open and ongoing discussion of all the feelings that arise, particularly sexual ones, and any fears. If any changes in the frequency of touch or type of touch occur this must also be discussed. Lastly, and perhaps surprisingly considering the amount of thought and preparation that has to take place, if touch is to be used therapeutically, the touching must be part of a spontaneous and genuine response and not an act or a technique. This will only be the case if therapists are acting within their own theoretical and ethical convictions. If this is the case then touch can be used safely by experienced and trained therapists as an effective tool of healing for some clients.

6

Social Situations and Friendship

It was mentioned in the previous chapter that touch gives the therapist an additional role as physical caregiver. It also can signify fondness. This can be confusing for a client and may raise the question of friendship. Many situations arise during therapy where actions that are part of a normal friendship enter the therapeutic relationship and these must be handled most carefully. In many of these situations there is also a conflict for therapists between their professional and personal selves. Frequently they have to balance the reasonableness of the request against the likely effect on the therapeutic task.

A different issue, but also involving a balancing act between politeness and therapeutic knowledge, is whether one should accept as clients members of current clients' families or their friends. These issues form the heart of this chapter.

Social situations

Some social situations that arise for a therapist and a client occur by chance and range from meeting on the street, in a theatre or other places of entertainment to being invited to the same wedding or other social event. It is always possible that a therapist and client have friends in common without realising it. Other social situations could arise because the client wants their therapist to be present at an important event in their lives, such as a wedding; a birthday, housewarming or retirement party; ordination; graduation ceremony; or to visit them in hospital. On at least one occasion a client's family wanted me to be present at the funeral of the client, knowing that I had had a significant role in her life. This also happened to Sue Wheeler (1996). Other social situations that may arise are an invitation from a client to join them for a meal, or an offer of a lift in their car if they pass their therapist waiting for a bus. A parallel dilemma exists for the therapist if they pass their client waiting on a cold, wet, winter morning. Should they offer their client a lift?

In every section of this chapter and in Chapters 4 and 5 decisions about crossing boundaries set to contain the client and the therapy are governed by the therapist's theoretical orientation. Psychodynamic therapists working from a relational paradigm and humanistic therapists are more likely to try both to offer consistency and yet to respond to clients' requests, than therapists with a strict psychoanalytic training. This is equally true when considering how to handle social situations. Social situations are of concern because they threaten the confidentiality of the relationship and also because they are open to misinterpretation, turning the strictly business relationship into a dual relationship; maybe only for an hour or two – none the less this can be confusing. This could be detrimental to a client, particularly if they believe a friendship is being offered, which is then not available. Obviously a social meeting can be very provocative.

Chance meetings will take place whether a therapist is working in a large city or a small town but they are even more likely to occur if both the therapist and client live in a small community, such as a small town or a rural community or a small, tight-knit social group of people. The latter is often the case for gay and lesbian people wherever they live. Since therapists know that chance meetings are possible, that there are professional rules, and that they have theoretical reasons for behaving in a certain way, the onus must be on them to have thought about how they will handle such situations and to clarify this for clients. If they do not do so clients have every reason to be aggrieved and hurt. More than one client has talked of their hurt when a previous counsellor had 'cut them dead' in the street, having not pre-empted such an occasion by discussing it beforehand. It is wise, therefore, to talk to clients about how such a chance meeting should be managed as soon as there is a mutual agreement to work together. It is equally important to check with a client how they felt after a chance meeting.

First and foremost it is the responsibility of the counsellor to maintain the confidentiality of the existence of the relationship between them and a client. This means that clients must be in charge of whether they acknowledge that they know their counsellor if they meet. I always agree with clients that I will follow their cue and only smile in response to a smile from them and warn them that if they do want to acknowledge me I will exchange social niceties but will not engage in conversation with them, nor introduce them to anyone who is accompanying me. If I realise during a session that a client and I are likely to be at the same event, I tell them that I expect to be there and again discuss how we should manage this.

Some therapists would not attend an event at all if they knew that a client was going to be present rather than create an awkward situation; other therapists would insist that their client does not attend such an event, particularly when the client is in training as a therapist and so might wish to attend the same seminars. If I arrive at a social event, such as a party, and find that a client is there I actively avoid meeting them if it is at all possible. If it is impossible, I try to keep contact to a minimum. In such a situation the client may feel very uncomfortable about the presence of their therapist. This could spoil the party for them. With this in mind I try to slip away as soon as is politely possible. However, if, for instance the social event is a sit-down meal, the only polite action may be to sit as far away as I can from my client and make no fuss so as to maintain the confidentiality of the relationship for the client. One of the consequences of being a therapist is that one has to bear in mind one's clients' best interests and eschew certain situations; a different form of abstinence.

On one occasion I met a person at a dinner party whom I had already spoken to on the telephone and with whom I had arranged an assessment session, although we had not yet met. My mind ran overtime as I gradually realised that this person to whom I was being introduced was the same person. I decided to avoid contact with her and her husband as much as I could, though this was difficult because the group was small. My dilemma then was whether therapy was possible now that I had met both her and her husband and they had met my husband and me. This was one of the issues that we had to discuss before deciding whether to enter into a therapy relationship. In agreeing to do so we both knew it was extremely unlikely that we would ever meet again in the social setting and hoped that the one social meeting would not interfere with our therapeutic relationship. To this day I am not entirely sure whether it did make it more difficult or whether it assisted the therapeutic alliance.

Apart from these chance meetings clients do on occasions want their therapist to be present at a major event in their lives. In my time as a therapist I have been invited to a housewarming party, birthday parties, a retirement party, an ordination and a wedding. The reason for the invitation has been because clients believe that these major life events have been achieved because of the therapeutic work and they want to share their pleasure. Assuming one's theoretical orientation allows one to attend, there are other considerations. These are the nature of the relationship with the client, the 'developmental' stage of the client, the type of social event, and the effect on the client of one's refusal or acceptance and one's presence or absence.

Some therapists never accept any invitation. If this is not one's theoretical stance and professional association's rule then the first consideration is whether one's attendance or absence would harm the client. It is unlikely that one's absence would do harm but initially the client might not understand why their invitation was being refused and be very disappointed or annoyed. The reasons should be made clear and any feelings of the client explored, made sense of in the context of the client's life story, understood and accepted. In the case of parties one's presence could compromise the confidentiality of the therapeutic relationship unless, when asked how one knew the host or hostess, one answers rather vaguely that they are a friend. This response immediately illustrates the problem, because the therapist is not a friend in the conventional sense. Friendship is discussed further later in this chapter. A better and more truthful answer is that you 'met on business'. Quite apart from this difficulty it is likely to be very uncomfortable for a therapist to attend a party at which they know no one but their client. In many ways it would probably feel false to be present: this, combined with the ambiguity of whether one is a friend or not, makes it very unwise ever to attend a client's party.

There is much less ambiguity in relation to a wedding. Firstly the therapist is likely to be pleased for the client that s/he is getting married and will be happy to celebrate this with them. Secondly one can attend the wedding and maintain anonymity by simply slipping in at the back and out again as soon as the formal ceremony is over and not attending the reception. It is equally easy not to disclose one's identity at an ordination or a degree ceremony, because generally a large number of people are being ordained and there are a lot of guests so one can easily remain incognito. In both these instances there is no need to chat to anyone, nor does one need to know anybody; one is simply sharing in the joyous ceremony.

The decision of whether one needs to attend or not to convey one's delight in the client's achievement is a difficult one. Clients at some stages in a therapeutic relationship would like their therapist to be present in the same way they would have wished their parents to be present. It will be enough for some clients to understand this and for their therapist not to attend, but for other clients who have suffered early deprivation and so cannot feel their therapists' pleasure, this will only be felt as further rejection. They may begin to know other people's pleasure if their invitation is accepted and they see their therapist at the event; but even then they may not know. However, it may be a worthwhile experiment to attend: the shared joy may result in considerable growth for the client because the affirmation is seen to be real and one's presence is unlikely to do any harm. There is a small group of people, perhaps more often seen in private practice than any other therapy setting, who are lonely and solitary. Often their therapist has got to know them better than any one else ever has and the client may feel closer to them than to anyone else. It would be almost inhumane not to attend a celebration that they invite one to. This is an instance of the responsibilities that accrue if one offers therapy to certain groups of people.

The dilemma of whether to pick a client up or accept a lift from a client also arises as an inevitable result of establishing a relationship. At times there is a very difficult balance between ordinary human decency and therapeutic appropriateness. There can be no hard and fast rule about what to do. What is essential is to discuss with the client the consequent feelings they have, whether you picked them up or not or whether you accepted or refused a lift from them.

A totally different type of social dilemma arises if a client asks one to visit them in hospital. This is a situation where one has to know the client well and be very mindful of the relationship. This is illustrated in two scenarios.

Mary has counselled Jim for about a year when he is suddenly admitted to hospital. Jim's wife rings to cancel the session and asks Mary if she would visit him in hospital as he is going to be in for at least three weeks. Mary feels uneasy as she is asked to do this and remembers that Jim is very unhappy about his marriage and critical of his wife, but wishing to be polite she says she will do so. When she goes to see Jim she feels very uncomfortable and is suddenly aware that he has strong erotic feelings for her. She leaves as quickly as possible. Jim never resumes his counselling after leaving hospital despite a letter from Mary suggesting a date for this.

In this case Mary should have taken her uneasiness to supervision before deciding whether to visit Jim in hospital. It is likely that she would have recognised that there was already an erotic transference and probably decided that a card to Jim would have been better than a visit.

Anne had been Jean's therapist for four years. Early in the counselling relationship Jean had had a mastectomy but had recovered well. Anne had visited her in hospital a couple of times and knew that this had contributed to Jean's trust of her. About two years later Jean developed secondaries in her lungs, which did not respond to treatment. It rapidly became clear that Jean's cancer was terminal and she only had a few months to live. Anne, in consultation with her supervisor, started to visit Jean in hospital. This deepened the relationship between Anne and Jean and both were aware that this support enabled Jean to come to terms with her terminal illness.

In this second scenario Anne had no misgivings about visiting Jean, indeed she knew it was the humane thing to do, and in consultation with her supervisor she decided that it was more beneficial to the client to visit her in hospital than to stick to the preset boundaries. She and her supervisor also explored the likely consequences of visiting Jean before Anne did so.

Anne continued to take her relationship with Jean to supervision and was greatly helped with her feelings as Jean became progressively more ill.

It is very difficult to conduct a therapeutic relationship when a client is in hospital because all the normal set-up is missing. One is likely to be meeting in a busy ward, so privacy, confidentiality and intimacy are all compromised (Wheeler, 1996). If one's client is mobile then it is worth asking for a private room but if not, one has to make do with meeting at the bedside. Once both the client and therapist have got used to the strange meeting place it is likely that both parties will become so engrossed that the necessary therapeutic work can be done: not least because the therapist is probably there precisely because there is work to be done. If it is saying goodbye, this will be done. This was a very profound exchange for Wheeler (1996).

If a client dies, as in the case described by Wheeler, there are further dilemmas. A therapist is still duty bound to maintain the confidentiality of the therapeutic relationship and yet members of the family may know of one's connection. If one is asked to the funeral does one go? Sue Wheeler decided to attend but not to go to the reception where she was to be guest of honour. This would have compromised the confidentiality of the therapeutic relationship, if she had had to explain who she was to members of her client's family. She 'attended the funeral, unobtrusively sitting alone at the back and slipping away through a side door at the end'. This would have satisfied the family and also enabled her to mark the ending of her client's life and help her to begin the grieving process.

Counselling people with whom one has connections

On occasions friends and even family of a therapist ask if they can come to them for counselling, or if the therapist will see another member of their family. They may do this because there is no problem in formally consulting friends or family on professional matters in other areas of expertise, as mentioned in the first chapter. It seems common sense to ask for help from someone whom one knows and already respects and trusts. The received wisdom is that this is a bad idea because it introduces a dual relationship and complicates the therapeutic relationship. If one works in an agency this is not a problem because one can ensure that they see someone else. If one works in private practice then one has to decide what to do. Most people understand the inappropriateness of this as soon as one points out how different a therapeutic relationship is from any other professional relationship. A client generally sees a therapist regularly and for a lot longer than a doctor, dentist, accountant or any other professional and they are likely to share very intimate material that they may never have told anyone else.

However, on at least one occasion a friend has asked if she could see me for a few counselling sessions and even after I had pointed out all the inherent difficulties in combining a counselling relationship and a friendship she persisted. After much thought and discussion with my supervisor I agreed, for two reasons. I knew that I had been asked because I was trusted and she knew she was accepted by me. This was very important for someone who had a deep conviction that no one accepted her. I also knew that she was very troubled and talked to few people. My hope was that a 'good' experience with me would enable her to ask a therapist she did not know for help a little later. This is what happened and our friendship was not affected adversely. We both knew what belonged to each relationship and that certain topics that came up in counselling were 'out of bounds' for our personal friendship. This is one instance where my credibility in my own community was critical in attracting clients and where giving primacy to relational ethics rather than following prescriptive rules set out in ethical codes seemed the right action. There are many instances where counsellors from small, tight-knit communities, such as bisexual, gay and lesbian groups, will see friends or friends of friends and apply exactly the same reasoning and procedures to make the therapeutic relationship possible.

Friends also ask for a professional opinion on such matters as how to manage an awkward family or work situation:

Peter and Jane were friends of Judy, who was a counsellor. Judy knew they were worried about their son Tom, who frequently suffered from depression. One day Peter phoned Judy and asked if she could recommend a counsellor for Tom, who lived in the West Country. Judy suggested they contact BACP, who she knew would send, by post, names of counsellors in that area. About two years later Peter rang up one day and asked if he and Jane could come and get some professional advice from Judy. They were still worried about Tom, who had seen a counsellor for about a year but had now stopped. As far as they knew this was a negotiated ending, not a sudden withdrawal by Tom. They couldn't understand why this had happened when they felt that he was no better. This was a considerable dilemma for Judy. Did she refuse on the grounds that she did not want to mix work and pleasure? On the other hand it was reasonable for Peter and Judy to ask for advice without needing to go to a counsellor themselves. It was also a straightforward request on the telephone rather than picking her brains whilst out walking together. After some thought Judy decided that it would not jeopardise their friendship to suggest they came to her house and spent an hour or so together wrestling with how Tom might be best helped.

Not all counsellors would solve this problem in the same way. The important thing is to do what seems appropriate to the relationship, and not to get into a situation where one feels exploited or resentful.

Current clients sometimes ask a therapist if they will see a friend of theirs or give a friend their therapist's phone number. Clients will also ask if another member of their family might join them at sessions or come separately for therapy. All these situations can complicate the therapeutic relationship, and each one has to be considered on its own merits and in the light of the context in which one works. Some agencies have strict rules about this and also may use an assessment interview before placing a client. If a potential client specifically asks to see a named therapist, the person who is the first point of contact, who may be a receptionist or an assessor, can enquire how they know the name and suggest whether this is appropriate or not. In private practice the therapist has to handle the client's question of whether they would see a friend of the client for therapy. It is important to establish what type of friendship exists. Are they acquaintances, business or close friends? It is also helpful to enquire why they want to share their therapist with someone they know and whether they would feel comfortable doing this. Sometimes clients have not considered the consequences but felt compelled to ask because of the nature of the relationship with the 'friend'. They often feel relieved when the request is thought through and they can think about whether the likely consequences are acceptable. I would not knowingly agree to be therapist to a close friend of a client because I find that knowledge of one can contaminate my relationship with another, particularly if the relationship between the two becomes soured. I find it hard to keep the knowledge in separate compartments in my head. This will not be everyone's difficulty. With other levels of friendship I would try to decide on the grounds of the best interests of my current client. One cannot always do this if a client simply gives one's phone number to a friend. This is one reason why it is sensible to ask someone enquiring about therapy how they heard of one's name. If one only discovers later that there are overlapping relationships then the confidentiality of each relationship means that one must not divulge the existence of one to the other. In this situation one has to find a way to keep the two relationships separate in one's head, which can be a problem. It will also be essential to discuss the difficulties in supervision.

Decisions also have to be made if a client asks if their partner can either join them for some sessions or come separately for therapy. There are similar dilemmas if it is another member of their family, such as an adult child, or a brother or sister. There are no hard and fast rules but as with any other request it is important to understand both the basis and the timing of the request; to explore the consequences for the current client; to check that the partner or family member would not feel that the process was biased in favour of the original client; to check that the current client understands that the therapist will not divulge information, gained during the original one to one sessions, to the new party.

Last but not least, the practitioner has to feel comfortable with the change or they will be unable to work effectively. I would also advise both the therapist and client to think about it and in the case of the therapist to take the question to supervision before deciding jointly with the client what is in their best interest. My personal motto is, 'If in doubt, don't'! Undoubtedly there are times when it is in the best interest of the client to arrange joint sessions, but this is only true if both parties really want to work together. It is unlikely to work if the family member is only there out of curiosity! If this is the case it will rapidly become obvious.

Friendship

There is always a danger that actions of the therapist can be misleading and be misinterpreted as signs of friendship, when this is not the intention. A therapeutic relationship is most unusual and may be unlike any that the client has experienced before. It contains elements of friendship such as trust, mutual understanding and respect and yet it is not a typical friendship. Lynch (2002) suggests that a pastoral relationship is only effective if it contains elements of friendship. He draws on Aristotle's understanding of friendship to try and understand the complexity of different types of friendship. Aristotle described three categories of friendship: utility, pleasure and virtue. In a friendship of utility 'the relationship is maintained because it is in some way useful to both parties'. A business relationship is a typical example. The two people are there because of self-interest and neither party has to be a virtuous or pleasant person: they simply have to understand the rules of business. Generally this type of friendship ceases as soon as the business connection stops. A friendship of pleasure exists when people meet because they enjoy each other's company or have an interest in common. The people have a friendship because they share an interest in dancing, gardening, football, theatre, walking and so on. They will like aspects of each other but will not be kindred spirits. The friendship will almost certainly stop once the two people no longer find each other's company congenial or one of the pair stops the shared activity, or if one of them moves away. The friendship would only continue if there were something else they also share or find to share. A friendship of virtue is much deeper and arises because both parties have a 'fundamental love and regard' for each other. This takes time to develop and is built up as each person's knowledge of the other grows and deepens. The friendship is likely to have useful and enjoyable parts but it is not founded on these. Self-interest is likely to be reduced and the prime motivation is a high regard for one another, which is based on mutual understanding and respect. Aristotle saw this as the ideal relationship.

At the start, when a client and therapist agree to begin work together, they are initiating a business relationship and therefore a friendship of utility. It is unlikely to be a friendship of pleasure but it is not uncommon for clients to believe that it could be, or is, a friendship of pleasure or even one of virtue. This is probably because a therapeutic relationship, particularly a long-term one, does not fit neatly into any of the three Aristotelian categories but is a 'moderated friendship' (Lynch, 2002) with elements of both a friendship of virtue, such as mutual regard which deepens over time and a friendship of utility. It is important that the therapist does not mislead clients and keeps the relationship as a friendship of utility as well as helping clients to understand the confusing nature of this friendship, which is akin to a friendship of virtue.

Despite a therapist taking considerable care to keep the boundaries of the therapeutic relationship clear, some clients, who are very lonely and do not make deep relationships easily for fear of commitment, yearn for a friendship of pleasure or virtue with their therapist. This is probably because the moderated friendship of therapy is deeper than any friendship they have ever had, and may have lasted a long time. This desire may be particularly difficult to handle because however much one person believes that the friendship is one of virtue, it is not that unless it is reciprocated. This can be a very hard truth for some and at times so hard to bear that a client chooses to end the relationship rather than feel the pain. Others prolong the relationship so they can enjoy some closeness and feelings of friendship, thinking that this is better than nothing. Obviously the therapeutic dilemmas are rather different in these two responses. In one instance the client needs to be encouraged to stay and work through their disappointment; in the other the ending has to be faced. The question common to both is: can one learn as a result of a therapeutic relationship to make friendships of pleasure and virtue? For some the answer seems to be that they can only learn to make friendships of pleasure.

Some clients do ask if there can be a friendship when therapy ends. For some therapists this is never a possibility because they believe that the transference relationship is never totally resolved, the power dynamics existing during the therapeutic relationship continue and the therapy should be about freeing the client to pursue friendships of pleasure and virtue within their natural networks of friends and acquaintances. Other therapists are prepared to experiment with their client on what is possible after therapy has finished. This experiment must not be undertaken unless both parties really want to see if there actually is a potential friendship of pleasure to be shared. It is wise to let at least three months elapse between the end of therapy and embarking on a new relationship, because both parties may find their feelings have changed as the intensity of the therapeutic relationship has waned. It is also prudent to discuss the planned change of relationship with one's supervisor and to decide how much time should elapse between the end of therapy and exploring the possibility of friendship. Sometimes it takes much longer than three months before the client is confident that they do not need to refer to their therapist to maintain their self-esteem; sometimes the start of a friendship with the therapist is a denial of an unresolved dependency and is therapy under another name. If this happens it is likely to be draining to the therapist and certainly will not be two-way, as a genuine friendship should be.

I have explored the possibility of a friendship of pleasure with three or four clients. Each time I have made the decision to do this because I have genuinely liked the person, and after discussions with my supervisor have been as certain as I could be that the therapeutic journey was complete and the dependency and idealisation no longer present. In two instances after about three years the client has let the friendship drop, and I have felt this was the right decision. Clearly the friendship of pleasure was not possible, and the feelings of friendship had arisen from a mutual interest in the therapeutic endeavour and not anything deeper. When this interest dissipated, as the therapy receded, there was no longer a common interest and therefore no basis for a long-lasting friendship. It is also possible that I had been wrong about the completion of the therapeutic journey and the friendship had been formed to maintain a surrogate therapeutic relationship until the client felt able to end the relationship.

There are instances when it is necessary to stop a therapeutic relationship to allow a friendship to develop:

Mark had attended an evening talk on bereavement organised by his local church. The speaker was a counsellor called Jean. She had been invited to speak because both the vicar, Stephen, and his wife, Margaret, were close friends. About a year later Mark began to think about therapy for himself and decided to approach Jean. They met for an assessment session, agreed that his presence at the talk a year ago would not have a detrimental effect on the therapeutic relationship, and decided to work together. Some time later Stephen and Margaret separated and Margaret came to live close to Jean. Margaret and Jean then began to meet quite regularly. At much the same time Mark's marriage also began to founder. Gradually Jean became aware that Mark often visited Margaret after his therapy session and a relationship was developing between them.

It was difficult for Jean to decide when the time was ripe to mention her concerns about the overlapping relationships; but when it became clear that Mark had fallen in love with Margaret she thought that she must say something. Jean decided that she had to discuss with Mark the difficulty of his deepening relationship with Margaret in relation to her own friendship with her. Together they decided that the best thing to do was for Mark to move to another therapist so that all three of them could allow the relationships to unfold. Mark did not want to change therapists even though he could see the common sense of doing so. Jean's conviction that it was right and that a friendship could emerge helped him in his decision. Mark moved to another therapist and began to meet Jean socially when he accompanied Margaret. For a time it was difficult for all three of them but after about a year all awkwardness disappeared. Mark did marry Margaret and all three are now close friends.

Occasionally a therapist will be aware that in other circumstances their client could be a friend of virtue or even that there is a friendship of virtue present. In my 20 years as a therapist I have been aware that I felt much closer to one or two clients and that this was not a countertransference response related to the clients' need to be special. The traditional view of psychoanalysis is that the therapist has to be abstinent and neither allow the friendship to develop, in the belief that the therapeutic relationship is what the client has contracted into and is what will be most helpful; nor terminate therapy so that the relationship can develop, because the transference relationship and the inequality in power will persist and affect the subsequent relationship adversely. A difficulty arises if the client senses that there is a friendship of virtue present and there is every reason to suppose that clients will know what their therapist is feeling. Heyward (1994) in *When Boundaries Betray Us* puts this very clearly:

> It is not just the healer who realizes what is happening in therapy. Whenever a genuinely creative moment of relational engagement happens, both persons are being touched, moved, changed, in the moment – *and both know it*. The client, if she [sic] is intuitive and empathic, often knows as much as the therapist about what's going on between them. (Heyward, 1994: 32)

Heyward was certain that her therapist was feeling that there was a 'mutual relationship' (friendship of virtue) and she wanted to end therapy so that a friendship could evolve. She writes passionately of the hurt and the emotional damage she suffered when her therapist refused to acknowledge that a 'mutual relationship' had developed between them and did not agree to end therapy so this friendship could develop. Her therapist's reasons for refusing to allow the relationship to change are not known, because she did not take up the invitation from Heyward to explain her actions. However, Heyward believes that the reason was that her therapist's professional body prohibited this.

Many psychoanalytically based therapists believe that the power dynamics are such that the 'transferential dynamic cannot be transformed into a bond of human intimacy' (Heyward, 1994). Heyward disagrees (as do I), believing that this transformation is possible and that she was not in the grip of a transferential neurosis. She suggests that it is fear that inhibits this transformation. There is always a danger that psychodynamic therapists play a game in which the client's behaviour is pathologised as an unresolved transferential neurosis and the client's intuition is ridiculed. More generally there is always a danger that any professionals, in this case therapists, feel they 'know best'. With this in mind, it is important to pay attention to what Carter Heyward has to say. It would appear that the denial of her intuitive knowledge was very damaging to her and she felt that 'abuse can result from a professional's refusal to be authentically present with those who seek help'. In addition, 'such abuse can be triggered as surely by the drawing of boundaries too tightly as by a failure to draw them at all'. This quotation from Heyward seems an apt end to this chapter for it summarises the dilemma posed, which is how tight the boundaries should be.

7

Non-Sexual Dual Relationships in Training, Supervision and Research

The majority of experienced senior counsellors and psychotherapists have two roles, if not more, within the profession and thus dual relationships can and do arise. Apart from working as therapists, they may well be trainers, supervisors or researchers, or even have all three additional roles, and they may also manage a training course or a service offering counselling in the voluntary, public or commercial sector. In addition, if they are active in the profession locally or nationally they may serve on a committee with a current or ex-supervisee or an ex-client or trainee. I recently went to a meeting in a large conurbation with about 70 therapists. I attended because it interested me, but also to meet my annual Continuing Professional Development requirements. Amongst this group were two current clients, one current supervisee, three past supervisees, two past clients, one client of one of my supervisees, at least five people who had attended short courses I had run, several people with whom I had been on committees and, of course, every therapist who attended was a colleague and many were competitors for clients and supervisees. In this chapter I will address the problems and management of the overlapping roles of therapist, trainer or supervisor and the dual relationship problems that arise because therapists are members of a relatively small professional group.

The other major question discussed in this chapter is how to conduct research when the material for the research has to be supplied by current clients; thus two relationships are set up with the client – as therapist and researcher. A parallel situation occurs if a trainer or supervisor is collecting data for research from trainees or supervisees respectively.

Training

There is no doubt that the role of trainer is very difficult and perhaps the most complicated professional role that any therapist has to perform. Trainers first and foremost have a teaching and evaluative function. The evaluation involves not only an academic assessment as in any other course, but also, unlike most other forms of training, the emotional maturity of the student has to be assessed. The reason for this is that an individual's emotional maturity affects their capacity to be an effective therapist. Thus trainers will become aware that a student needs therapy to explore some personal issues and without this therapy they are unlikely to pass the course. It can be very tempting to combine the roles of trainer and therapist to assist a student, and some students will expressly ask trainers for therapy, since they already know and trust them.

Apart from introducing and examining critically at least one theory, if not more, underpinning therapeutic work, counselling and psychotherapy courses have to teach counselling skills, so the trainer has to observe and assess this work. The trainee therapist has also to do a considerable amount of supervised client work and is likely to have some supervision and case discussion of this work with course trainers. This gives the trainer a role as supervisor as well.

A trainer has therefore to be very aware of the possibility, or even the temptation, of forming dual relationships with trainees. The questions are: should a trainer ever offer a trainee therapy? How does a trainer maintain impartiality in the evaluative system when they are also therapist? How does a trainer manage to train and supervise client work and give the trainees a safe environment in which to explore their mistakes?

Some courses do allow trainers to be the therapists of the students they teach; some even insist on this. There are two reasons for this. Firstly it ensures that students receive therapy from practitioners whose practice is totally coherent with the methods being taught. Secondly it puts the trainer in the best position to judge whether a student is emotionally mature enough to become a therapist. If this is the approach it will be essential that all the students receive therapy from course tutors and that measures are taken to prevent favouritism. If it applies to just some students, fear of collusion may arise, with some of the other students being anxious about or believing that the students in therapy with trainers are favoured. Of course collusion can take place, and again steps need to be taken to prevent this happening. But the opposite could arise, with a student believing that they were penalised because their trainer-therapist knew too much about their emotional world and was failing them because of this; and this would be the correct thing for a trainer to do if they sincerely believed a trainee-client was not yet sufficiently emotionally mature to be a therapist. Simultaneously a student who felt penalised by having their trainer as a therapist might believe that a fellow student with a therapist external to the course was in an advantageous position and passed the course because the course tutors were unaware of any emotional problems. This type of conflict can result in students deliberately concealing information about themselves for fear it will be used against them, whereas in a more normal situation it would probably be freely available. It is essential that trainers are aware of the conflicts that their course structures can cause and try to be as open and transparent as possible. When anxieties and fears arise for students they must be taken seriously. If they are not, trainees can become enormously angry with both the course and the trainers; so angry that they lodge a complaint with the college or the professional association. Sometimes these complaints are more than justified, but some are vengeful attacks or vexatious complaints arising from sheer rage because fears have not been addressed.

A further problem, which may occur when course tutors are also therapists, is that the students are likely to have only a small number of therapists available to them. This can have a number of consequences, which need to be thought about by the course organisers. The dynamics of the group will be affected, possibly detrimentally, if some trainers have more members of a year group in therapy with them than others. It is not uncommon for a group of students to see some trainers as 'good' and others as 'bad', and some trainers will be better teachers than others, with the result that there may be considerable competition between students for therapy from one or two of the trainers. This could be counteracted by deciding to limit the number of students from any cohort that a trainer can have in therapy, but it might result in considerable resentment against the students who were first to get assessment appointments with a popular trainer. Another consequence of only trainers being available as therapists to their students is that it will almost certainly give them a very limited choice, which could result in some students feeling they had to choose a trainer/therapist whom they thought was second best. In general at the beginning of therapy a client must choose a therapist they really want to work with, although some people can never be so positive. The reasons for this are that the formation of a working alliance is necessary before any in-depth work can be done; and that if the relationship is stormy later, the client knows that it began with a positive desire to work with that particular therapist. The changes in feelings can be used to help a client understand themselves and their relationships. A third difficulty occurs if the trainee feels unable to work with the trainer or if the trainer has to cease offering therapy temporarily, because of a personal difficulty such as a bereavement, or permanently because they believe the relationship is no longer helping the trainee. In all these instances it may be very difficult for the trainee to move to another course trainer for therapy and the maintenance of confidentiality may also be jeopardised. It is the course tutors' responsibility to be aware of the type of conflicts that can arise for students and to check with each other that students are being neither penalised nor preferred because of dual relationships. To ensure transparency, a therapist who is independent of the course could be used to facilitate such discussions.

I mentioned earlier that trainers' principal role is evaluative. This may not only relate to whether a student has passed or failed a course, but in the case of psychotherapy training, the course trainers also control the gateway to the profession. The successful completion of a registered course automatically allows someone to register as a psychotherapist. This gives trainers immense power that is open to abuse. Two methods are used to counteract this: a trainer/therapist will absent themselves from the room and the decision-making process; or they declare a vested interest and remain in the room and take part. In both these solutions the probity of the practitioner is relied upon and collusion is assumed not to occur. Unfortunately there are dishonest individuals who can manipulate such a system.

There are also difficulties for the trainer/therapist when in the role of therapist or in the role of trainer. When in the therapist role it is likely that the trainee/client will bring course-related material to the therapy. Should a complaint about way the course is run, or the teaching of another trainer, or difficulties with another student, or a comment about oneself as a trainer, be treated as reality or transference? It may be that as a co-tutor one knows the truth behind the difficulties of a trainer about whom the trainee/client is complaining. This must not be divulged and attention should be given to what is happening in the room between the therapist and client. When in the role of trainer the trainee may bring material that makes one's role as a tutor more difficult: for instance, if the client/trainee reveals that another trainee has cheated or is working unethically. This type of material would at the least be distracting and at worst it would be very hard to resist being drawn into the issues the information reveals. Overall the trainer/therapist will have considerable difficulty in keeping the 'out there' of the course separate from the 'in here' of the therapeutic relationship.

It is possible for course organisers to take great care either to prevent or successfully to address all the complications mentioned when a trainer has the dual role of trainer and therapist. The therapist and trainer of a client can also address all these issues in therapy. However, there is evidence from the complaints received by BACP that this is often not done successfully, and some students have been damaged by the conflicts. It is the major reason why BACP when they introduced the *Code of Ethics and Practice for Trainers* in 1985 insisted that 'trainers should not accept their own trainees for treatment or individual therapy for personal or sexual difficulties should these arise or be revealed during the programme of training'. I was trained in psychotherapy on a course which did allow students to be in therapy with trainers, though not all students took this option. My therapist was a tutor and decided not to take part in the decision-making process, which meant that I had one less examiner on the course and the person who knew me best could not speak up for my strengths or weaknesses. I have always thought that this disadvantaged me, though I may be biased!

The question that remains for course organisers is how to assess emotional development and maturity if trainers are not therapists to their students. This has been addressed in two ways. One is to have a list of names from which the students select therapists, who then report to the course on the progress of the trainee. This again introduces a dual role for the therapist and can lead to defensiveness on the part of the student, which will affect the therapy. However, such a process can be used very well, with the student taking part in an appraisal process with the therapist and being able to discuss the report and understand more about themselves. Some courses prefer not to introduce such a dual relationship and therefore keep the therapy separate from the course and do not seek reports from the therapist. If they do this then another way, such as a personal development group, has to be found to foster and assess emotional maturity. Normally a therapist who does not take part in the day-to-day training, and thus has a measure of independence, facilitates such a personal development group. The students are informed of the criteria used to assess personal development at the beginning of the course and then work with the facilitator and the group to set themselves goals to be attained and to assess whether these have been reached. Whilst the facilitator has the final say on whether a student has met the personal development goals set and therefore passed this component of the course, the student should have a realistic assessment of their own development and not be surprised at the outcome.

Another conflict of roles arises for trainers because an essential part of training is counselling practice, which must be supervised by an experienced practitioner. More often than not the supervisor is external to the course. This counselling practice is a major source of learning for students and issues of technique and the handling of difficulties that arise need to be discussed in class. However, this can lead to the trainer acting as a supervisor, when the trainee already has a supervisor for this work, and can result in a piece of client work being 'over-supervised'. It can also be confusing for a trainee when their own supervisor and the trainer disagree about how to manage a therapeutic issue. It is important for trainers not to consider themselves as supervisors analysing a piece of work with a specific client, but rather as mentors discussing broad issues.

There are courses where the trainers are also supervisors because it is considered essential that the trainers assess directly the therapeutic work being done by a trainee, rather than rely on the opinion of supervisors external to the course. Here trainers are deliberately given a dual relationship and are assessing not only the academic work of a trainee but also their counselling practice. This can work well for some trainees but not for all. Some trainees feel too threatened by the assessor role of the trainer/supervisor to present work that they believe might be poor practice or about which they are unsure. The whole point of a good supervisory relationship is that the supervisee should feel secure enough to explore all their work, whatever its perceived or actual standard, and know that they are not going to be judged as failing. Obviously this cannot be guaranteed when a supervisor is also assessing whether one's work is of a high enough standard to pass a course. For me this possible insecurity of some trainees, which is likely to affect their work detrimentally, far outweighs any benefit there is to the trainer in having client work presented directly. Indeed there are reasons to believe that the course assessments are likely to be more impartial when senior practitioners in the locality are involved. These people are comparing the trainees with qualified practitioners whom they also supervise and therefore offer good quality assurance.

It is often necessary for a trainer to think about potential dual relationships before or at enrolment. The following exercise illustrates some of the dilemmas.

Exercise 7.1: Dilemmas for a therapist/trainer

Read the following case study and then consider how Fiona should tackle the dual relationships that would arise if Peter were to apply for a place on the course she tutors.

Peter had been in therapy with Fiona for over two years. Fiona was not only a therapist but also a trainer on a local course. Some way through therapy it became obvious that Peter was very interested in therapy and was beginning to wonder whether he could train as a therapist. Fiona also thought that Peter would probably make a good therapist and was satisfied that he was not thinking about training either to copy her or because he idolised her and the profession. She knew from what he said that the course he was interested in was the one on which she tutored and one course requirement was for trainees to be in therapy throughout their training.

Fiona began to wonder what she should do.

In Exercise 7.1 there are a number of issues that would arise for Fiona, the therapist/trainer, and would need to be thought about and probably discussed with a supervisor. If Peter does not know she is a trainer on this course should she tell him or let him find out? Should she suggest to him that he applies for another course, or even insist that he does that?

Should she suggest that he does not make an application for the course until their therapeutic work is complete? If he applies for the course and is accepted should she suggest they finish their therapeutic relationship and he move to someone else before he starts the course? If they do this, how long is the optimum time between ending therapy and starting on the course? What are the additional complications if the only course available to Peter is the one Fiona teaches on?

The actions therapists in this situation would take would be very varied and affected by the therapeutic relationship, the setting, the theoretical model of the therapist and the two individuals involved. However, the most important decisions will be related to whether there would be harm to Peter or his fellow students if a dual relationship were created. There is no reason to suppose that Peter would necessarily know that his therapist was also a trainer, and even if he did, that he would be as aware as his therapist of the difficulties that would or could arise if he enrolled on a course on which she taught. It would therefore be important for her to establish what difficulties he envisaged and then to look at what he had not considered. For Peter it might seem a good idea to have his therapist become his tutor as well. However, it is unlikely to be good for his fellow students or for the dynamics of the group if Peter is perceived to have a special relationship with a tutor. So for the good of the group Peter should not be in therapy with Fiona once he starts on the course, but even stopping therapy before the course started would still leave a closer relationship between the two of them than between Fiona and the other students. In the best of all possible worlds, Peter should enrol on a course with which Fiona has no involvement and continue in therapy with her until the work is complete. In some situations this is not a realistic solution because there are very few courses available or only one course in a particular modality. Should this occur then it would be essential to have a considerable time gap between the end of therapy and the start of the course. A suitable gap might be one year, but for some this would be unnecessarily long and for others not long enough. The gap needs to be long enough for Peter not to need to believe he has a 'special' relationship with Fiona, or to play on their past relationship. It would be important for Fiona to meet Peter after the gap and discover how they both felt and then for Fiona to discuss the issue with her supervisor before making a decision. If Peter does then join the course it will be essential for him and Fiona to acknowledge to the group their previous relationship.

There would be other instances where course tutors and members have a prior knowledge of each other, an earlier relationship, or an existing one. It is conceivable that a tutor will only know at registration that someone they know quite well has been accepted on a course on which they are tutor. In this instance the dual relationship exists and has to be handled. Again the relationship must be openly acknowledged and then an agreement reached on how this is handled. One possible way would be for every effort to be made to avoid any social meetings during the course. However, this would be impossible if one member of a sexual partnership wanted to attend a course tutored by their partner. It is perfectly possible that no alternative course is available, because one does not exist locally or in the vicinity. Can the partner never receive training because their partner is the trainer? This seems an unrealistic and unfair solution. Where this occurs it is again essential that the existence of the relationship is public knowledge; that all the students have a forum in which to discuss their fears and difficulties with an independent person, who has the power to demand changes if there are genuine difficulties; and, as in other instances of possible conflict of interest, that any assessment is seen to be conducted impartially.

Sometimes students who have completed a course ask one of the trainers if they will now become their therapist. It may be flattering to be asked but it has to be remembered that there will almost certainly be a lot of unworked-through issues. Trainers on a course may well be aware of such things as idealisation or vilification by a trainee or unnecessary compliance or unctuousness, but it is not their task to address this transference behaviour, though they will have to survive it! These are examples of obvious behaviour but many feelings could either be hidden from the trainer or be unconscious for the student. Whatever these feelings are they will build up during the course because they are not addressed. A further complication is that during the course trainers may well be more open about themselves than they would be if they were in therapist role. Overall, the ex-trainee is likely to be carrying a lot of unresolved issues related to the course, quite apart from life issues, to the therapeutic relationship. For these reasons I would not advise anyone to take on an ex-trainee as a client.

I have been asked to do this on two occasions. Both times the people had attended a short course of six days on counselling skills put on by their employers. The first time the trainee asked me during the course. I suggested she waited until well after the course ended and see whether after a break she still wanted to start therapy. She rang me after three months and asked if she could become a client. After an assessment session and discussion with my supervisor I decided that we could work together. One decisive factor for me was that it had been such a short course and the other was that there was no obvious transference. Nowadays I would say that this should be a very strong reason not to offer a therapeutic relationship. We worked together for about five years but it was quite the most difficult work I have ever done, because the dependency needs, which did not emerge until several months into the therapeutic relationship, were so pronounced and very hard to resolve. With hindsight it is clear that the dependency issues must have been there during the course and at the assessment sessions, but they were hidden from me until the client felt safe and a strong working alliance had formed. In the other instance the ex-trainee rang me at least five years after the course, with no contact in between. Again I picked up nothing at assessment that indicated that it too would be a very fraught therapeutic relationship. I should have been more aware that if someone had attended such a short course and still remembered me after such a gap there would be very strong transference issues, even if they were undetectable at assessment.

I have also discussed the wisdom of taking on ex-clients with trainers who run much longer diploma courses. In their experience it is very rare for trainees to ask for a change in role, which suggests that most people have decided that it is not a good idea. The few who have been asked and who have accepted an ex-student as a client have found that it was an extremely difficult therapeutic relationship, just as I had found when the course was short. This suggests that at the very least the therapeutic relationship will be much more complicated with an ex-trainee than most other clients. This is not necessarily a reason to avoid such a relationship, but forewarned is forearmed. I would not agree to be a therapist of an ex-trainee again.

Supervision

Supervisors hold a very powerful and privileged position in the profession of counselling and psychotherapy. Powerful because they are entrusted with the continuing quality assurance of the profession; and privileged because as senior practitioners they are chosen by other therapists to oversee their work and trusted to explore it critically, whatever its standard, in great detail. Inevitably supervisors also set an example of how practice issues such as dual relationships are handled ethically. Dual relationships are a frequent issue for supervisors, because the number of senior practitioners who are both experienced therapists and trained supervisors is limited. Many supervisors also work as trainers and therapists and serve on professional committees. In addition many practitioners have friendships of utility and/or of pleasure, if not of virtue, with other therapists in their area. This may not be a problem in a very large urban area, such as London, but is likely to be a major one in smaller cities, towns and rural communities.

In this section the questions related to dual relationships are: should someone simultaneously be therapist and supervisor to one practitioner? Should one change from being therapist to supervisor or vice versa, or from trainer to supervisor, and if so how long should the gap between the two relationships be? Should a therapist supervise the work of a practitioner whom they know socially and work with on committees? Should therapists allow themselves to become close friends or even enter into a sexual relationship with a supervisee? Should therapists enter business relationships with their supervisees?

There are a few psychotherapy courses where therapy and supervision are combined. The rationale for this is that any difficulties that arise with a client are going to be directly related to personal, emotional issues of the trainee-therapist. Once the trainee-therapist understands their emotional blocks and these have been resolved then they will be able to work on the problem with their client. Whilst this is true it does mean the focus of the work tends to be much more on the trainee-therapist than his/her client. One of the strengths of separating therapy from supervision is that in the therapeutic relationship the focus is on the trainee-therapist and only indirectly on the client, and in supervision the opposite is true. This enables the therapist to be as vulnerable and needy as is necessary at that particular time and stage in the therapy, without needing to or having a reason to put their needs on one side and attend to the client. It also ensures that clients' needs are not competing with the therapist's needs. Each has due time and recognition. I have acted jointly as a supervisor and therapist on one psychotherapy training course, but more often have kept the roles separate. I have no doubt that the client is the major focus of attention when the roles are separated. When they are combined, particularly if the therapist is new to therapy or dealing with very deep emotional problems, it is very hard to give the client any time at all, let alone a fair portion of the time. For this reason I agree with BACP, which has always insisted that supervision is 'intended to ensure that the needs of the clients are being addressed and to monitor the effectiveness of the therapeutic interventions' and is 'not primarily intended for personal development' (BAC, 1996a). The combining of therapy and supervision is a dual relationship, which is to the detriment of the client and the quality of the therapist's work and therefore should be avoided.

If the roles of therapist and supervisor are separated then the more experienced practitioners are likely to have to consider the request to be the supervisor of someone who was previously in therapy with them. For some who believe that transference issues are never totally resolved in therapy, it is unacceptable to change roles from therapist to supervisor. It would be seen as a way of maintaining the therapeutic relationship under another guise. A strong counter-argument to this would be that a supervisor who had previously been the supervisee's therapist would be well versed in the issues likely to interfere with a piece of work with a client and can swiftly draw the supervisee's attention to these without reverting to the therapist role. An additional safeguard to ensure that the focus of the supervision remains on the client work and does not drift back into the old therapeutic relationship would be to agree that if any serious personal issues arise, which interfere with the client work, the supervisee will seek therapy with someone else. Whether a supervisee has been a client in the past or not, this is a good agreement to have from the start.

The change from supervisor to therapist appears to be much simpler because any power and transference issues that may have arisen in the supervisory relationship are a legitimate concern of the therapeutic relationship. Likewise any feelings related to the change are there to be explored. However, in many cases it would not be simple at all nor appropriate to change, because one's manner as a supervisor might be very different from one's manner as a therapist. In general I am much more informal and friendly to my supervisee, who is also a colleague, than I would be to a client. When working as a therapist I divulge much less personal information than as a supervisor. It would be very confusing for both parties to change roles. If it were viable to change roles then the main issue would be to ensure that the old task of supervision does not creep in and interfere with the therapeutic relationship. If it does, this needs to be addressed. An example would be when client work is being used to avoid working on something frightening or horrifying.

If one has no objections to changing role then the question is: what is a suitable gap between the two relationships? This was touched on when discussing training earlier in this chapter and also in Chapter 6 when discussing the change in relationship after the end of therapy. There are no set rules about the length of time between any two relationships but it would be unwise to move straight from one into the other, and it should never be assumed that this move is automatic. In the case of a client becoming a supervisee there is considerable risk of the supervision simply being a continuation of the therapy without sufficient time for the outcomes of therapy to be resolved. The received wisdom is that it takes at least three months to adjust to the end of therapy and work through the loss. For some people it will take considerably longer. It is essential that the supervisor examine the issues first with the potential supervisee and then with their supervisor before making a decision about introducing a changed relationship.

Supervision relies on two people trusting one another. This is likely to be the case if there was a good working alliance during therapy. It also relies on there not being too great a power differential, though inevitably there will be one. But if it is exaggerated by an inappropriate attribution of power to the supervisor by the supervisee, this will make the joint endeavour of exploring the client work in detail very fraught. The supervisor will know from the previous therapeutic relationship whether issues of idealisation have been worked through. Another prerequisite of good supervision is that supervisees need to be able to discuss differences of opinion, and accept guidance and judgements without being too defensive and, should they become defensive, be able to notice this and explore the reasons. Here again the supervisor will know from the previous therapeutic relationship the emotional maturity of the ex-client who wishes to become a supervisee. It will be clear from this that a supervisor (ex-therapist) of an ex-client, who after the termination of therapy wishes to become a supervisee, has a lot of information to enable them to make an assessment of whether a change in relationship will work, provided there has been sufficient time since the therapeutic relationship ended for the loss to be worked through. If there is a change in role, from client to supervisee and therapist to supervisor respectively, it would be sensible for the new relationship to be considered a trial, which is reviewed after a few months to check that both parties find the change satisfactory and in particular to check that the focus of attention is upon the supervisee's clients. When making this agreement it should be made clear that the new relationship ends if either party is unhappy with the change.

If the change in role is from supervisee to client I would again suggest a break between the two relationships of at least three months so that there is a deliberate discontinuity. It is also important to explore with one's supervisor the reasons for contemplating such a change with a supervisee. This should help ensure that the decision is made for good reasons and the new task is seen as different. It would also be wise to review the consequences of the changed relationship after a few weeks and to set the same conditions about the arrangement being satisfactory to both people.

A trainer who is approached by an ex-student for supervision is also likely to have a lot of information about a student's ability and maturity, at least at the point when the course was completed. It is possible that a student may attribute too much power to a trainer. Unlike a therapeutic relationship, there is no necessity for this to be addressed by a course tutor during a course. This means that this will need to be assessed in the exploratory meeting between the ex-student and trainer before any agreement is reached about changing role. Again it is essential for the supervisor (ex-trainer) to discuss the possible pitfalls with their own supervisor before any change in relationship occurs. A likely problem would be the pull to change the nature of the supervision from a discussion of the work with a client to a more didactic tutorial. There is a place for some teaching in supervision, particularly with a relatively inexperienced therapist, but it should be a minor component. As with changing from therapist to supervisor, some time must be allowed to elapse between the two relationships. There is no rule about this, but again a break of at least three months would be wise, and like every other changed relationship, the new one should be reviewed after a few months and there should be a let-out clause for both people in the initial contract.

It was mentioned earlier that practitioners who act as supervisors are usually the most senior therapists in the area; this means their number is small and inevitably they will become involved in overlapping relationships with other therapists in their locality. This leads to five interrelated questions. Can one supervise someone one meets socially or works with on a committee, or should one avoid accepting as supervisees people with whom one socialises or works? Can one join a committee on which supervisees are already working? What does one do if someone one works with on a committee or occasionally meets socially asks one to be their supervisor? How does a senior practitioner find someone for their own supervision who does not have overlapping roles with them? What does a supervisor do if they do meet a supervisee at a professional meeting or socially?

If it is accepted that it is inevitable that as a supervisor one will have dual relationships with other therapists in one's location then these relationships need to be managed, or everyone has to go much further afield to find supervisors. I believe it *is* inevitable because, as in most professions, there is a pyramid structure, with few people qualified or eligible because of experience to be supervisors. If the senior people were to refuse to serve on committees or to let their supervisees work on committees on which they already serve, or to be supervisors of practitioners they know from a variety of common contexts, then the profession would be seriously affected. If they avoid meeting a supervisee socially, then their lives will be seriously depleted. The practitioner is entitled to a social life without the abstinence required of them in their relationships with clients. Whilst in theory it might be possible to go further afield it may not be practicable for a number of reasons. Travelling further for supervision would result in less time for client work and lower earnings in some instances and lower caseloads in others. In some parts of the country the therapists would have to travel unreasonable distances for supervision. For instance if one worked as a therapist in the Orkneys or Shetlands the nearest supervisor with whom one did not have a dual relationship might be in Inverness or even Aberdeen, which would involve a ferry trip and a long drive or a plane flight. This type of problem does not only exist if one lives on an island; when living in more rural areas such as parts of Cornwall, Wales or Cumbria unacceptably long journeys might also be necessary. It is for these reasons that it is more realistic to manage dual relationships rather than to ban them.

It is possible to manage these relationships first of all by discussing at the initial session how any meeting should be handled so both people are comfortable. It is also important to discuss candidly either the probable or the actual effect that meeting socially or professionally has on the supervision. If either person is finding it difficult then this is a reason to stop, but if both are comfortable with the overlap then it is reasonable to continue. There is a greater danger of the supervision becoming less objective, or even collusive, perhaps resulting in the supervisor not being sufficiently challenging or even turning a blind eye to poor practice or malpractice, if there is a dual relationship. This would be serious for the clients and the profession, but if both supervisor and supervisee are alert to this and regularly review their work with a particular eye to the possibility of collusion it can be counteracted. The supervisor ought also to bring the issue regularly to his or her own supervision so that everyone is alert to the possibility. Another method is to invite a third person to join the supervision periodically with the specific task of looking for any evidence of collusion. It may also be wise to change one's supervisor regularly even if the new supervisor is also someone with whom one has a dual relationship. At least different personalities are involved so it is unlikely that the same issues are being ignored.

It is very difficult for senior practitioners to find supervisors locally for their work with whom there is no previous or existing relationship. The most important consideration is that neither the clients nor the supervisor is harmed by a dual relationship. It is again unreasonable to expect a practitioner to travel long distances, so management is necessary and the same procedures have to be undertaken to prevent collusion. An alternative, which I have found helpful, is to have a supervisor with a different theoretical orientation and trained in a different part of the country. Such a person can be found in a large city but probably not in a small town or a rural area. I would not recommend this to an inexperienced therapist, but supervisors are by definition senior practitioners.

In most communities it is likely that a supervisor will meet a supervisee at professional meetings, which often have a social component, or at a social event for they will often have friends in common. This is another situation which is better managed than banned. Here again it is sensible to discuss how this should be managed at the initial session and then check out after each meeting how it actually felt for both parties. On some occasions one will also meet the partner of the supervisor or supervisee and the impact of this has also to be checked out. I have never found these overlaps difficult, perhaps because trained professionals are handling these problems so that both parties can have some areas of their lives uninhibited by their work.

It is more likely that a supervisor and their supervisee could get to know each other well enough to want to have a deeper friendship, than a therapist and client. Should this occur, it is essential to stop the professional relationship, discuss it with one's supervisor or some other independent consultant and have a pause before exploring a new relationship. There may be a transference relationship present as well, which would impede a friendship, but this is not necessarily the case. There can be no difference between two work colleagues realising they like each other and want to get to know each other better and two therapists wanting to do this. It is also perfectly possible for a supervisor and supervisee to be attracted to each other sexually. It is of course equally abusive for a supervisor to make uncalled for sexual advances to a supervisee as for a therapist to make them to client. However, there is no reason why two therapists who work together in a supervisory relationship should not find they are attracted to each other and want to have sex, explore the sexual relationship further and even ultimately to decide to marry or live together. The only proviso would be that they terminate the supervisory relationship before exploring the sexual and amorous relationship. It would also be wise to have talked the issues over with someone independent of either party such as one's supervisor of supervision.

Another conceivable dual relationship between a supervisor and a supervisee would be the possibility of going into business together. In supervision one might discover that one had overlapping interests. If this happens it is again wise to terminate the supervisory relationship before making any business agreements. It would also be wise to discuss the issues with someone who is separate from the issues and able to be impartial. This might be one's supervisor. Indeed a key to any desire to change the nature of a relationship from supervision to something else is not to act in haste and to consult before doing anything.

Research

Any practitioner conducting research using their own clients, trainees or supervisees, whether past or present, immediately creates a dual role between themselves and these people. Even if they do not use their own clients they are likely to view them in two ways: as therapist and as researcher. The research question could leak into the therapeutic relationship and distort the process. On the other hand a good practitioner always carries a sense of exploration and enquiry into any professional relationship between themselves and their client, trainee or supervisee. In addition a competent practitioner should be monitoring and evaluating their work, if not actually conducting research. From the point of view of the profession, research needs to be done with current and past clients to accumulate evidence of the efficacy of counselling. This makes the dual role of practitioner and researcher inevitable, though stated this way it sounds as though research is a chore rather than the fascinating pursuit it actually is. As with all other dual relationships this has to be managed to ensure that clients are neither exploited nor damaged by the experience.

Nobody should be expected to take part in a piece of research without it being explained, so that the consent is informed. Both BPS and BACP give guidance to their members on conducting research. BPS publishes 'Ethical Principles for Conducting Research with Human Participants' as part of their *Code of Conduct, Ethical Principles and Guidelines* (1998). It has a brief guide on issues of informed consent. BACP publishes an information guide titled *Ethical Guidelines for Monitoring, Evaluation and Research in Counselling* (1996b) which clearly outlines the steps that must be taken to ensure that clients have the necessary information to give their consent freely. Yet there is a sense in which it is impossible to know the actual impact of being a part of a research sample until the research has been conducted. There will be both obvious and hidden reasons why clients consent to take part. They may believe, however much they are reassured, that their therapist will be annoyed with them if they refuse, will not be as interested in them, or will not give them such 'good therapy'. Obviously such behaviour would be unethical, but when clients have a past history of punishment for not complying with an authority figure's request this can be transferred to the therapeutic relationship. Or someone may refuse to be part of a piece of research and then fear or perceive punishment for their action. The therapist should be aware that this is unethical practice, but why should a troubled client know or believe this? If researchers need a representative sample of their clients or indeed want to use them all for research then these types of difficulty will arise. There is no reason why these difficulties should be damaging to clients if they are explored and their origins understood. Such exploration could even be therapeutic. McLeod (1999) suggests that an additional safeguard both for the client and the therapist/researcher is to ensure that clients have the name of an independent arbiter that can be contacted if they feel under pressure to partake in the research or if they feel concerned about any of the arrangements.

Another difficulty for the therapist/researcher is that some clients will try to second-guess the required outcome of a piece of research in an effort either to please or punish. This may not be detectable but if it happens it will not help the research, so there should be a caveat in any discussion of the outcomes. Another caveat is that it is very hard for a researcher to remain impartial and therefore it may be very difficult to remove one's own bias and really interpret the results properly. McLeod (1999) suggests that a way to avoid this is to collect data and then have it analysed by someone else.

There are marked differences between the compassionate involvement of the therapist necessary to form a working alliance and the compassionate distance of the researcher needed for an effective research alliance and to maintain impartiality. It may be extremely difficult to move between these two positions and very confusing for the client. This suggests that research with a current client should involve only the completion of questionnaires at various points before, during and after the therapeutic relationship. Logically, research with current clients involving interviews needs to be done with people who are currently in therapy with someone else and who should be found by methods such as advertising.

Research also needs to be conducted with past clients. The most important consideration is whether reopening the relationship will be harmful to the ex-client. Some clients, even when the therapeutic relationship has been good, have moved on to a different phase of their life and are able to say 'no' to the request. However, others may say 'yes' and then find they are drawn back into the relationship. It also has to be remembered that an uninvited letter or a phone call that arrives out of the blue from one's ex-therapist may feel invasive, though it is easier to handle a letter than the telephone. In the latter case an instant rather than a considered response may appear to be being demanded. On balance it is probably better to conduct research with one's own ex-clients using questionnaires and to conduct research needing face-to-face interviews or focus groups with people who are not one's own ex-clients.

If one conducts an interview or leads a focus group the compassionate distance may lead some of the research subjects to ask for therapy and thus ask for a dual relationship. If they are already in therapy with someone else then it is not ethical or professional to encourage them to move. However, if they have concluded a piece of therapeutic work with someone else then a decision has to be made. I think it is unwise to move from being a researcher to a therapist for the same reasons that it is unwise to move from trainer or supervisor to therapist. In all three instances the persona adopted when training, supervising or conducting research is different from that of the therapist. The behaviour when conducting research, such as the level of openness and friendliness, may make the transition to the new professional relationship very difficult and minimise or dilute the therapeutic endeavour.

8

Challenging the Limits: Dual Relationships in Small Communities and Pastoral Relationships

Dual relationship problems also arise in small communities, and were mentioned in the last chapter in the context of professional groups. They may be small for geographical or professional reasons, such as small rural communities or professional groups; for lifestyle reasons, such as a commune or religious congregations; for specialist need reasons, such as the deaf community; for survival reasons, such as a group who are treated prejudicially or even persecuted (examples are gays, lesbians, transgender and bisexuals and members of immigrant communities); for isolationist reasons, such as some minority religious groups who fear contamination by cultural norms; and for employment reasons, such as a company who employs an in-house counsellor both to train staff and to offer short-term therapy. In many of these instances dual relationships arise because the members of the community do not want to go outside the group, so there are few counsellors to undertake the roles of therapist, trainer and supervisor. This desire to remain inside the group also makes it inevitable that the therapist knows the client socially. A major question in this chapter is how to handle such dual relationships.

A closely associated problem is that of imams, rabbis, priests and lay-readers who work as pastoral carers and counsellors with members of their own faith community and have to find ways to manage these dual relationships.

Small communities

The particular issues for small communities have been mentioned several times, but the topic is important enough to gather the main ideas under one heading. The different types of small communities have some common characteristics. Three of the groups, those formed for lifestyle, survival or isolationist reasons, are communities of trust, although some groups will have a profound mistrust of the rest of society. In many cases there is good reason for this, because members of the gay, lesbian, bisexual and transgender communities, of minority ethnic groups and of exclusive and minority religious sects are frequently discriminated against if not actively persecuted. Because of this insecurity they frequently prefer a therapist to be a member of their own community, whom they trust, who has credibility within the community and is thus held in high regard. It is also understandable for a potential client to want a counsellor who not only is empathic to their situation but also understands from first hand experience what it is like to be a member of a minority community which suffers discrimination. If therapists refuse to be active in their community, then they are in danger of being seen as standoffish, of losing credibility and possibly denying their own membership of the minority group. They also risk becoming isolated from the community to which they belong, which is of itself an emotionally unhealthy position for anybody whether a therapist or not. The dilemma is: how does a therapist who is a member of such a community remain part of it and ensure their own emotional health and also practise their chosen profession outside the community when the majority of requests for therapy come from within it? This makes it extremely likely that therapists from these communities will have multiple relations, even if they live in a large city where there are a number of networks, because the loyalty will be to the local trust community and is unlikely to be generalised to all minority groups. However, when engaging in multiple relations the practitioner has to manage the boundaries.

Therapists from sexual minority communities where non-monogamous relationships are common often find complex boundary situations with 'overlapping links between clients, ex-lovers, current lovers, friends of ex-lovers, friends of clients and so on' (Gabriel and Davies, 2000). Awkward social situations also arise. Gabriel and Davies give as a case example a lesbian therapist attending a 40th birthday party given in her honour. Part of the fun is that she does not know who is invited. I shall name the therapist Linda. Amongst the eight guests is a client, Sarah, who is deep in conversation with Naomi who had been the therapist's lover until about six months ago, when they had parted amicably and had not maintained contact. The therapist knew Sarah had a lover, but not her name. She also knew that the lover did not know that Sarah was seeing a therapist. As an additional complication the therapist was aware that an erotic transference had been developing towards her that had not yet really been explored. When landed in a situation like this many questions would arise in a therapist's head. Should one leave the party? Does Sarah know that Naomi had been her therapist's partner? Will Naomi disclose at the dinner party that Linda, the therapist, had been her lover? Will Sarah reveal that Linda is her therapist? Will the other guests reveal incidents in her life which she would rather Sarah did not know? And so on. This is but one example of the many awkward situations that can arise when therapists belong to a small community. Another example is given in Exercise 8.1.

Exercise 8.1: Meeting a client socially

Peter is a therapist. He is invited to the celebrations of a friend and ex-lover, Martin, who has recently formed a partnership with Guy. Peter and Martin have not seen much of each other recently because Martin has been working abroad. When he arrives at the celebration Peter recognises one of his clients, Michael, and gradually realises he is Guy's brother. During therapy Michael often speaks of his brother's exploits and says that he is HIV positive. Peter also knows from Michael that Guy has more than one lover at the moment.

What feelings, thoughts and questions might go through Peter's mind? What would you do?

Gabriel and Davies (2000) give a much more challenging case example of a therapist, who has a positive attitude to saunas and 'cruising' and 'see(s) nothing 'pathological' in enjoying or even celebrating casual, uncomplicated sexual expression'. He is taking part in an 'exciting group sex scene in a dark room of a gay sauna', when he realises that the person he is masturbating is a client. The client has discussed in therapy his ambivalent attitudes to sex, though the negative feelings predominate. None the less he is drawn compulsively to casual sex. At no point has he mentioned any sauna that he has attended. It seems to be chance that they both attend the same place on that particular day. This type of situation, as with any ethical dilemma, will lead to many feelings, thoughts and questions. Feelings such as:

- guilt if buried shame at 'being found out' is revived;
- worry about implications for one's career;
- anger that one's social time is 'invaded' by clients;
- frustration if one decides to leave the group sex.

Thoughts and questions such as:

- Did the client recognise me?
- Could this possibly psychologically damage the client?

- Will this result in a complaint to the professional association?
- Should I leave now, or stay and move somewhere else?
- Should I speak to the client before I leave or move?
- What was said about boundaries and meetings in the original contract?
- I must speak to my supervisor.
- How do I work through this with my client if he continues to work with me, or has the relationship been irrevocably damaged?
- I have breached the codes but they are general and do not cover casual sex in specific cultural settings.
- Would it be considered unethical if neither of us knew the other was involved and it stopped as soon as we realised?
- I do not think this was exploitative or am I simply justifying my action? The codes are particularly concerned about exploitation.
- Could this chance encounter assist the client in being able to accept himself, or is this also justification? (Adapted from Gabriel and Davies, 2000)

This may be a particularly challenging example of the problem of a dual relationship occurring unexpectedly but it does illustrate that one cannot be too careful. It is important to make initial contracts that are based on intelligent predictions of meetings which might arise and that do indicate how unexpected meetings will be handled. As a general principle this is equally true for all relationships where there are boundaries to be managed when client work and community overlap.

This type of overlap is also found when therapists live in a small community, a large distance from other villages, towns or cities. These communities are not necessarily communities of trust but there are reasons why multiple relationships are frequent if not inevitable. In such geographically isolated communities it is not reasonable to expect someone to travel hundreds of miles to find a therapist, supervisor or trainer with whom they have no prior or current relationship. This results in two types of multiple relationship, those with personal overlaps and those with professional ones. Thus a client may well also service one's car or run the local shop, or be the partner, child or close friend of a previous or current client. Professionally one's therapist, trainer or supervisor may also have had another professional role previously or be someone one meets regularly socially or professionally, or indeed be a good friend. The smallness of the community means that practice has to be different than in a large town or city. An example is that it is easier to maintain a client's privacy if the counselling room is in one's house rather than in an office. This is because people come to a therapist's house for a large number of reasons whereas there would only be one reason to arrive at a therapist's office. Excercise 8.2 gives an example of the type of problems that arise for therapists working in a small community.

Exercise 8.2: Managing dual relationships in a small community

Pat is a counsellor in a small village with its own cottage hospital. She is admitted to hospital for observation, having collapsed the previous day. About four hours after she was admitted and when she is still feeling very shaken, she realises that a current client has been admitted and is being taken to the next door bed.

What feelings and thoughts might go through Pat's head? How would you handle such a situation?

Members of the deaf community have very similar problems of overlapping boundaries as members of small rural communities. This is because relatively few hearing people can also sign and few people who are deaf are trained as therapists. Again it demands great care in managing the boundaries. This has been written about in some detail by Guthmann and Sandberg, 2002.

Therapists and welfare managers trained in counselling often have problems with overlapping boundaries when working in commercial organisations or large public services such as hospitals or universities. These are not trust communities but the employers expect their employees to be multitasked and thus overlapping relationships occur. In both types of organisation the welfare managers or counsellors are expected to run short courses on topics such as stress management or an introduction to counselling skills, and offer their employees short-term counselling on work-related issues. In addition welfare managers may have a considerable number of non-therapy roles with people who have attended courses or received one-to-one therapy. For instance they may have to act as an advocate for an employee with financial difficulties or who faces disciplinary action, or help someone negotiate redundancy terms. It is also highly likely that they have to attend meetings at which past, current or potential clients and their managers or staff are present and in which details of past, present or future clients are discussed. Small organisations would not be able to afford extra welfare managers or counsellors to manage these overlapping relationships, nor is it reasonable to forbid a client to come on a stress management course, or the welfare manager to attend a meeting, because there have been other therapeutic or non-therapy roles. Employers do not expect to make exceptions for counsellors and welfare managers, which often leaves these counsellors and welfare managers very stressed as they try to manage their conflicting roles. In Exercise 8.3 there is an example.

Exercise 8.3: Managing the dual role of counsellor and welfare manager

Carol is a welfare manager in a small company. The company is concerned about the level of absenteeism and has been cracking down on people going off sick. The Managing Director thinks that the people who have sick notes for stress have hoodwinked their doctors and are really malingering. She has been at a meeting where this was discussed and did state that stress is really debilitating and some of the working patterns of the company are stressful. She felt that she was not really being heard. A few days later she was asked by the Managing Director to visit John, who had been off work for two weeks suffering from stress. She feels very worried as she journeys to his house wondering how she can support and listen to John knowing that his employer does not believe he is ill.

What would you do in this situation?

To some extent a therapist working in an environment or culture where dual relationships occur also educates people in how to manage these boundaries. In the case of welfare managers it is important that they actively instruct their employers about therapy by producing information leaflets and running seminars on topics such as managing boundaries and the associated issues of confidentiality, and the ethical restrictions for a therapist. There is no reason for members of an organisation to know about the particulars of therapy any more than the therapist should know about the business. Both have to learn from each other.

In all these situations where multiple roles exist for valid reasons, the therapist has the major task of managing the boundaries in such a way that the client, supervisee or trainee is not harmed or exploited. The task for the therapist is to develop role fluency (Clarkson, 1995) so that the awkward boundaries, and perhaps totally new ways of behaving for the client, are managed realistically and respectfully. Gabriel (2000) suggests that anyone managing these difficult boundaries has to develop a vigilante approach to guarding the relationship boundaries and processes. Reiterating a point made earlier in this chapter, the therapist should have thought through the ways in which overlap might occur, so they are not surprised too often, and should already have developed strategies with which to manage most situations. Welfare managers know that people they have counselled might attend a short course, and vice versa. They also realise that they could counsel a manager one day and a member of the manager's staff the next day and that one may be dealing with issues about the other. Therapists working in small communities know that they will meet their clients in many situations and which activities they regularly undertake socially, recreationally, politically and spiritually. They also know that they are likely to have clients who have overlapping relationships with each other whether it be as friends, lovers or ex-lovers, spouses, children or next door neighbours.

In all these instances it is also important to check with a supervisor that one has been realistic about the likely difficulties. It would also be wise in some instances to make no decision about whether to work together at the first meeting, so that one can check it out with a supervisor before undertaking the work. A significant part of the first session needs to be spent exploring the acceptable ways of handling any relationships happening outside therapy. To a large extent the therapist will need to lead the discussion because s/he can predict at least some of the likely meetings. In the case of social events that both people want to visit, one solution might be to take it in turns to attend. A welfare manager might negotiate with clients that they do not attend any short courses during the counselling. However, it is probably impossible.to foresee every overlap so there has to be some general agreement about how to handle the unexpected. One approach might be to agree to behave as naturally as possible, not to divulge that there is a therapeutic relationship and to discuss the feelings and thoughts in the next session. In one sense the therapist is modelling how to separate different roles and how to maintain respect for and the confidentiality of the therapeutic relationship. It would be wise for the therapist to discuss any chance encounter with a client in supervision.

Discussion with one's supervisor is particularly important when working with two or more clients who are related to one another or who have had, or currently have, a relationship. One must not compromise the confidentiality of any of the relationships and yet one may have heard from one person something that materially affects the other. Unless it has been agreed that information can be shared, therapists must not divulge what they have heard. This means that one must find a way to segregate information from one client from that of another, and also monitor very carefully what one might say. This is not always easy, and for me almost impossible if I am seeing two people concurrently, who have a relationship with one another. I can do this if there is a gap of even a couple of weeks between finishing with one and starting with another, although I would recommend at least a month. The process of ending and the act of closure, rounded up with a supervision session, seems to enable me to metaphorically close the file. This stops me suddenly remembering information about somebody that I have worked with and I have to actively think about him or her to recall any information.

In many respects therapists who work in small communities, or where counselling and therapy are in their infancy, are very courageous because they are working at the edge. It is very unlikely that this type of work will have been discussed during training and not much has been published either. At times they will be uncertain whether they are practising ethically because the codes of ethics and practice have been so culturally specific that the special needs of minority cultures have not even been considered. Their work has challenged the profession to think more creatively and has resulted in the clause about dual relationships in the new *Ethical Framework for Good Practice in Counselling and Psychotherapy* published by BACP in 2002 to be drafted so that different working practices can be accommodated. The most important considerations are that the dual relationship is only undertaken if it is beneficial to the client and that the therapist is 'readily accountable to clients and colleagues for any dual relationships that occur'. I would add that in addition supervision is especially important when one is working on the edge.

Pastoral relationships

It is an essential and inevitable part of belonging to religious congregations and communities or other church organisations that members have overlapping relationships. The leaders (priests, rabbis, imams, ministers, chaplains, pastors, elders, etc.) are charged with the spiritual and pastoral care of their congregation, and pastoral tasks are frequently delegated to lay-people. An example of the latter is bereavement visiting in which members of the organisation support bereaved people for some time after the funeral. It would be considered reprehensible if priests refused to talk to and support church members with marital, family, work or personal difficulties and many would think it rather strange if they started by talking about confidentiality, time boundaries and fees; in other words, behaving like a counsellor. Indeed the ability of pastoral carers to be flexible in their responses is generally greatly valued (Lynch, 2002). There are dangers for the members of faith communities where the leaders are given and have power and are trusted implicitly, because some do abuse their power. Religious leaders are no different from other professional groups in that some members sexually and emotionally exploit people in their pastoral care.

Some leaders are trained as pastoral counsellors and some have a short course on counselling skills whilst at theological college, but many, when asked to do so, simply offer people pastoral counselling with very few sources of guidance. As a consequence they only face some of the boundary issues and role conflicts when either the church or organisation member or they themselves get worried, angry and upset. Lynch (1999) also suggests that a 'naïve theological emphasis on love' leads people to consider that 'well-intentioned acts of caring do not need careful critical scrutiny and that the use of clear boundaries in caring work is in some sense harsh and uncaring'. This attitude compounds the problems.

Lynch (1999) lists the following areas (which I have summarised) where there are potential difficulties; these can arise simultaneously when there is a blurring of roles:

- The counsellor's or client's experience of the relationship may inappropriately influence their interaction in other settings, e.g. strong positive transference means the client gives undue weight to the counsellor's opinion in other settings; or the counsellor acts on strong countertransference feelings from the therapy when meeting the client in another setting.
- The knowledge gained by the counsellor of the client in the confidential setting of the counselling is divulged in another setting because of uncertainty about what was learnt where.
- Behaviour appropriate to the other setting leaks into the counselling, e.g. the counsellor brings part of his/her role or opinions as a minister into the counselling relationship.
- The client's knowledge of the counsellor gained from outside the counselling relationship changes the focus of the counselling relationship.
- There is a potential for pastoral counsellors to seek intentionally or unwittingly to use clients to meet their own emotional needs, because many relationships are moderated friendships (see previous chapter) and involve half-intimacies. (Kunst, 1993, cited by Lynch, 1999)

One solution is to ban all dual relationships to prevent these risks being taken or indeed these role conflicts taking place. This does not seem realistic as it would ban the possibility of counselling help for some people who are in great need and unlikely to look for help elsewhere. It would also be out of sympathy with the ethos of support for one another, which is generally part of belonging to a community, who do 'worship, pray, work and socialise together' (Lynch, 1999). In some ways a community with prayer groups and other small gatherings can offer some people a healing experience, in much the same way that group therapy does. In both instances some issues about families can be worked through.

Even if one tries to make a distinction between pastoral care and counselling, as Lynch (2002) does, it does not preclude dual relationships from occurring. He distinguishes between the two on the basis of the approach to boundaries. Pastoral care is 'a more fluid type of work, often using "counselling skills" with a more flexible approach to the timing, location and the nature of the contract' than the pastoral counsellor would have. Pastoral counselling is based on the professional counselling model, with a clear contract and a consistent and transparent therapeutic frame maintained throughout the work. The purpose of the two is different, with pastoral carers being able to respond in flexible ways using counselling skills to give acceptance, support, understanding and empathy without encouraging people to explore their thoughts and feelings in depth, which is the task of a pastoral counsellor. This distinction would encourage someone to think about what type of work she or he was trained and equipped to do, but would not prevent dual relationships happening.

If it is accepted that dual relationships are part of pastoral practice, whether care or counselling is being offered, then they have to be managed just as in other areas of practice. Some dioceses, such as Oxford, have produced codes of practice to give guidance on this management, although the guidance is more directed towards ensuring that pastoral workers do not put themselves in positions where they are vulnerable to accusations of malpractice or tempted to exploit others. The *Code of Ministerial Practice* produced by the Diocese of Oxford (1996) specifically addresses issues of pastoral practice such as paying attention 'to the place and timing of a meeting and its duration'; 'whether a meeting is formal or informal in nature'; 'the atmosphere of the place of meeting'. It also warns against 'visiting someone late at night'; 'spending time with a child or children in a place separate from other people'; and 'a long-term pastoral relationship with one person in a partnership, when a significant part of the pastoral care focuses upon difficulties in the marriage/partner relationship'.

Pattison (1999) points out that such codes are a mix of ethical principles and specific prohibitions, but do not stimulate practitioners to think about their practice and take responsibility for it. Managing means 'developing a critical and reflective approach' to one's work and not being satisfied simply because clients have not been critical. There are many reasons why people might not give feedback. Good intentions and positive feedback do not guarantee good practice. Reflective practice led Ross (1999), a well-respected and experienced pastoral counsellor, to decide that the 'complexities of being both a counsellor and a priest' meant that he could not offer pastoral counselling to people with whom he had another pastoral relationship 'except in crisis intervention situations'. Implicit in this decision is that he offers pastoral care to people from other churches. This will not be everybody's solution, but is one that I would wholeheartedly support. Handling dual relationships means being aware of the pitfalls and actively guarding against them. Some of the possible risks were mentioned earlier in this chapter. In addition Kitchener (1988; cited by Lynch, 1999) identifies three sorts of role conflict, which make it more likely that the dual relationship will be damaging. These are:

- when there is a great difference in behaviour from one setting compared with another;
- when there is a great difference between the obligations and duties of one role as compared with another;
- when the professional helper's role has far greater power and prestige than the other role(s).

This knowledge is critical and must be part of the reflection when considering a dual relationship. Any possibility of damage is a contraindication to engaging in a dual relationship.

Some of the most complex dual relationships arise, and in my experience are least well handled, when religious groups set up their own counselling service, training their own counsellors. They frequently select all their trainers, supervisors and potential counsellors from members of the faith community. Their clients will also come from the same source. They may come from different meeting places or churches, but there is often a lot of overlap because they attend meetings and social events arranged for everyone in an area. In this sort of situation the counselling service needs to set very clear rules about reducing the overlapping relationships. At the very least it is important that trainers and supervisors from outside the group are found, and that counsellors do not counsel members of their own small faith community. External consultants must be used to ensure that there is very good supervision and that reflective practice is very much to the fore.

I stated earlier how vital reflective practice is, particularly when managing the complexities of overlapping relationships. An essential part of reflective practice is to ensure one's own emotional needs are being met outside one's professional work and, last but not least, having a supervisor with whom to discuss the pastoral work. Supervision is an important adjunct to therapy because one needs an impartial critic to challenge one's thinking and check it is not misguided or self-justifying. As yet, people working in pastoral settings do not often use this type of support.

Managing non-sexual dual relationships so that they are non-exploitative and cause no harm to clients, is the most challenging and the trickiest work that therapists do. It should not be undertaken by inexperienced practitioners. When non-sexual dual relationships are undertaken the practitioner has to be alert to the difficulties that role conflicts and blurred boundaries create for clients and use supervision to tease out the problems. Gabriel and Davies (2000) describe therapists managing dual relationships as boundary riders, who 'monitor and repair where necessary in order, as far as possible, to ensure security and safety'. The history of how this boundary riding has been managed and controlled will be discussed in the last chapter, together with some thought about how in the future it might be challenged by other cultures.

9

Learning from the Boundary Riders

The intention in writing this book was to find answers to various questions about how the psychological therapies have handled the role conflict and boundary issues created by multiple relations, some of which are indefensible and inexcusable, such as sexual relationships, and others inevitable, such as within small communities. One of the earliest questions in this book was, 'Is there a book to be written about that?' The answer is 'Yes', and a much longer one than I had expected. Behind this question was the belief of lay-people that dual relationships should not happen. The fact that this is too simplistic a view is the reason for this book. However, therapists need to hear the lay response because what this emphasises is their understanding that they share with therapists much more intimate and personal details than with any other professional. Information that is often so intimate that it is important to know that there is no possibility that it could be leaked by a mistake when meeting in another setting or when the therapist meets with someone from their circle. This must be remembered whenever creating a dual relationship seems to be the most appropriate response to a situation.

In this last chapter I will look at how the profession handled dual relationships at the start of psychoanalysis and as it developed and diversified into many different theoretical schools (e.g. Freudian, Jungian, Reichian, Adlerian) and allied professions (e.g. counselling, psychotherapy, counselling psychology). Alongside this development has been the gradual introduction of codes of ethics and practice, all of which have contained guidance on dual relationships. I will also examine the current situation and look at the handling of dual relationships in other cultures. These must be recognised if working with members of these cultures, but they also challenge our present ways of managing dual relationships, suggesting that the concern about role conflict may reflect a very Western way of thinking and is not necessarily appropriate to other cultures. It is essential to take this very seriously and re-examine our approach, because the rigid adherence to rules may not always meet our clients' legitimate needs.

Past to present

It will be remembered from the first chapter that Freud had dual relationships with members of his social group, his professional colleagues and his daughter. This was inevitable, because Freud discovered and developed psychoanalysis; and all of these people belonged to a relatively tight-knit social community and formed a small professional group. He therefore belonged to two small communities where dual relationships were inevitable, just as they would be today. The community in London where Jones, Klein, Winnicott, Little, Milner and Khan all worked was similarly small, again leading to the inevitability of multiple relationships. At least some of the group were medically qualified, which meant that professionally they were used to role conflicts and would not see these as remarkable in the psychoanalytic context. In addition in the first half of the twentieth century the general public assumed that professional people acted with integrity and probity. A characteristic of the British class system was that members of the upper and upper middle class were treated with deference and somewhat idealised, which they certainly did not always deserve. This is clear from the behaviour of Jung, Ferenczi, Reich, Perls, Khan and Rogers. All these men were very eminent psychoanalysts or psychotherapists and icons to their followers yet they had sexual relationships with female patients. I have not said the patients were sexually exploited and abused by these men, although I believe they were, because none of the women appear to have complained. This may reflect the change in the climate of public opinion between then and now. In Chapter 3 I gave some of the reasons why women who are abused do not complain, but I suspect that at that time the women would not have been believed. It is possible that they did not feel abused but rather were flattered. Whatever the women felt, if this type of behaviour came to light today the men would have had their membership of their professional body removed (as happened to Khan) on the grounds of sexual exploitation and abuse and bringing the profession into disrepute.

The inevitability of dual or multiple relationships with clients recedes as a professional group enlarges and as a larger number of people have received therapy. A cascade effect takes place as some patients recommend therapy to a friend or acquaintance from outside the original group. This results in an exponential growth so that fairly rapidly practitioners are not dependent for work on a small, local community of people. They can then begin to think about what constitutes good practice and make rules about boundaries with clients.

Counselling as a planned and organised activity first appeared in Britain in the late 1940s (Syme, 1994). By 1977 there was a sufficient groundswell for the British Association for Counselling (as it was then called) to be established. Seven years later, in 1984, the community was large enough to want to give guidance on practice with clients and start to make rules. In this year the first *Code of Ethics and Practice for Counsellors* was published. It was brief, with only 25 clauses (compared to 70 when it was revised for the first time in 1990), but three of these addressed boundaries. This is unsurprising when it is remembered that some people were committed to the formation of a counselling organisation because they were so concerned about the diverse standards of provision and the inadequate safeguards given to clients by some counsellors and counselling services. The first clause made counsellors responsible for setting, monitoring and making explicit the boundaries between a working relationship and a friendship (BAC, 1984: Clause 2.4), but did not ban dual relationships. A version of this clause has appeared in every subsequent revision of the *Code of Ethics and Practice for Counsellors*. It is at its most specific in the revision implemented in 1998, where it requires counsellors not only to set and monitor the boundaries but also to 'make explicit to clients that counselling is a formal and contracted relationship and nothing else'. This could be interpreted as a ban on dual relationships with clients but this is not directly stated. The second clause about boundaries directed counsellors to satisfy their own emotional needs outside their counselling relationships with clients (BAC, 1984: Clause 2.5). Here again this instruction has been included in each revision of the code. The final boundary clause made it clear that sexual activity with a client whilst engaged in a therapeutic relationship was unethical (BAC, 1984: Clause 2.6). This ban on sexual activity between counsellors and their clients, needless to say, has persisted until the present day.

A year later a *Code of Ethics and Practice for Trainers* (1985) was published with three clauses similar to those on boundaries found in the 1984 *Code of Ethics and Practice for Counsellors*. However, the parallel clause to 2.4 was extended, for obvious reasons, to ensure that trainers make the boundaries between therapy, consultancy, supervision and training explicit to trainees (BAC, 1985: Clause 1.5). There is also an additional clause directing trainers not to 'accept their own trainees for treatment or individual therapy for personal or sexual difficulties should these arise during the programme of training' but to refer them to 'an appropriate individual or agency' (BAC, 1985: Clause 1.8). This is the first time that a non-sexual dual relationship is prohibited. It is interesting that in the space of a year the association seems to have become aware that dual relationships can be a real problem. In general, additions to the *Codes* happen as a result of feedback from members and complaints that are received. This would suggest that there had been complaints from trainees, who felt abused by these unclear boundaries and dual relationships.

The introduction of this clause into the *Code of Ethics and Practice for Trainers* put BAC into conflict with many of the psychoanalytic training organisations, for at that time, and even today, many insist that a trainee is analysed by a training analyst who may be a trainer on the course. It will have created problems in some communities because a body of trained and experienced therapists suitable to be employed as trainers grows slowly, so that dual relationships with colleagues remains a problem for far longer, and will persist unless one lives in a very large city. Sixty years after counselling began to be practised in Britain and almost 30 years after the formation of BAC, London is the only place large enough for there to be no necessity for role conflicts or boundary issues to occur for practitioners choosing a therapist, trainer or supervisor.

Within two years a *Code of Ethics and Practice for the Supervision of Counsellors* was published (BAC, 1988). This was very similar to the two previously published *Codes* for counsellors and trainers, but places the onus equally on the supervisor and counsellor to monitor boundaries and distinguish between different activities. This is an important recognition that two professionals are working together and carry equal responsibility. It is recognised that 'on rare occasions' it is appropriate for the supervisor to change from supervising to counselling the supervisee. However, if this happens then the contract must be clear and it must not be done at the expense of the supervision time. This allows for an occasional dual relationship. One surprising omission is that engaging in sexual activity with one's supervisee is not forbidden nor even mentioned in the 1988 *Code*. This was not added until a revised code became effective in 1996. Perhaps the explanation is that there was a mistake in production particularly as there was a clause prohibiting it in the draft document.

The codes have all been revised, some of them several times. There have been three additions to the counsellors' code, which are of significance to this discussion of dual or multiple relationships. In 1990, when the *Code of Ethics and Practice for Counsellors* was revised for the first time, a clause was introduced forbidding exploitation of a client 'financially, sexually, emotionally, or in any other way'. This was subsequently added to the trainers' and supervisors' codes when they were revised in 1995 and 1996 respectively. The second addition of relevance was introduced in 1993 and referred to a counsellor's relationship with former clients. Counsellors were reminded that they 'remain accountable for relationships with former clients and must exercise caution over entering into friendships, business relationships, sexual relationships, training and other relationships'. If a change is being considered than this must be discussed with a supervisor and in particular consideration must be given to 'whether the issues and power dynamics present during the counselling relationship have been resolved and properly ended'. The third addition is found in the revision of the *Code of Ethics and Practice for Counsellors* implemented by the association in 1998. It stated that 'the counselling relationship must not be concurrent with a supervisory or training relationship'. It appeared logical to the authors of the *Code* to prohibit these dual relationships because it brought the *Code of Ethics and Practice for Counsellors* in line with those for trainers and supervisors. However, many people who worked in organisations were worried by this clause because it compromised them. It meant that they could not counsel someone who was attending a short course on topics such as counselling skills or stress. This was happening and the counsellors knew that their employers would not see the sense in such a ban, nor did the counsellors themselves. They were assured that the clause did not mean short courses, but many felt unsafe.

The revision of the trainers' code in 1995 brought in further prohibitions of dual relationships. Under a requirement for trainers to model appropriate boundaries there is an insistence that 'providers of counselling for trainees during the [training] programme must be independent of the training context and any assessment procedures'. In addition 'trainers must not accept current clients as trainees'; nor must former trainees become clients or vice versa, 'until a period of time has elapsed for reflection and after consultation with a supervisor'.

In the light of the changes in both codes, for counsellors and trainers, it will not be surprising to find additional guidance being added on handling role conflicts and boundaries when the supervisors' code was revised and implemented by the association in 1996 (BAC, 1996a). It was recognised that supervisors and supervisees would meet personally or socially but the *Code* cautioned against allowing this to 'adversely influence the effectiveness of the counselling supervision'. The other change was to ban a supervisor from having concurrently a counselling supervision and a personal counselling contract with the same supervisee.

It can be seen that over 14 years BAC had gradually developed its policies about dual relationships, although this term did not appear in any guidelines on practice until 2001, when a draft of the *Ethical Framework for Good Practice in Counselling and Psychotherapy* was published. Sexual dual relationships are always damaging and rightly are banned in every sphere of therapeutic activity. Some non-sexual dual relationships are also banned, i.e. whether someone is working as a trainer, therapist or counsellor they may only hold one role at any one time with the trainee, client or supervisee. It will be clear from Chapters 6, 7 and 8 that if these bans are followed in certain special circumstances then there is no therapy available to some people who would like to use it to understand themselves or the situation in which they are. The way these codes were worded put people who acted morally, responsibly and humanely to help these people in breach of the *Code* and therefore made them guilty of malpractice.

The ban on any sexual activity with a client would seem to be straightforward but in fact there has been much discussion about what is defined as sexual activity. Most people agree that this means not just penetrative sexual intercourse but also heavy petting, masturbation, fellatio and cunnilingus, but there is less agreement about where the boundary is between sexual activity and kissing and hugging (Bond, 2000). At times kissing and hugging will be a prelude to sexual intercourse and at other times simply an indication of affection. One only has to cross the English Channel to observe quite different rules on both hugging and kissing! This ambiguity makes it easy for someone to say that the act was not sexual and for others to suggest that the person is unaware of their unconscious motivations; but it makes it impossible to produce a clear definition of sexual activity. For this reason both the intention of the people involved and the interpretation of the receiver has to be weighed up. Obviously this makes therapists vulnerable to misunderstanding, so great care has to be taken to prevent this.

A particularly good example of the difficulty in defining what is sexual activity can be seen where a counsellor provides massage to an undressed client. This might be provided with all the usual protocols for remedial massage, such as those parts of the client's body not being directly worked on must be covered in towels and that the masseur must work fully clothed. It would be a challenging dual relationship to manage ethically and therapeutically. None the less there could be sufficient safeguards built in to limit or eliminate the possibility of the work being interpreted as sexual. What if the client remains naked or, as happened in the more experimental and freewheeling 1960s and 1970s, both the practitioner and the client are naked? At what point does the encounter become sexual activity? This type of incident has occurred and practitioners have taken opposing views. For some this is acceptable, albeit risky and challenging, if it can be justified therapeutically and is consistent with the therapeutic approach. For others, such behaviour is a breach of the prohibition on sexual activity and is too vulnerable to the interpretation that it is being undertaken for the practitioners own gratification and is thus exploitative. The boundaries between therapeutic appropriateness and sexual exploitation are a contentious issue and are likely to remain so. The general trend appears to favour caution, perhaps because our society is considerably more litigious than in the past. Those who work at the edge of this boundary do take a considerable risk.

Needless to say, all the other psychological therapies have published guidelines on conduct. I have presented those of BAC(P) because these show the gradual evolution of attitudes to dual relationships. The other three professional bodies of any size are the British Confederation of Psychotherapists (BCP), BPS, which has a counselling psychology division, and UKCP. Both BCP and UKCP are made up of member organisations, which publish their own codes following broad principles laid down by the parent organisation. Thus the broad principle in UKCP's *Ethical Requirements* (1998) is that 'psychotherapists are required to maintain appropriate boundaries with their clients', and ' they must take care not to exploit their clients, present or past, in any way, financially, sexually or emotionally'. An example of a strict interpretation of this by a member organisation, the Yorkshire Association of Psychoanalytic Psychotherapy, is: 'There must never be any sexual involvement between psychotherapists and their patients, supervisees or trainees. Social contact with patients should be avoided whenever possible', and 'Psychotherapists should never take on as patients, members of their own family or friends, colleagues or current supervisees'. Clearly this rigid approach does not allow therapists to make judgements about special circumstances, such as some of those outlined in Chapters 4 to 8, where I have advocated that there are times when dual relationships are justifiable, provided that clients give informed consent, therapists consult with their supervisors in the decision-making to check that their judgement is not impaired, and clients are not exploited or harmed in any way.

BPS adopts a less prescriptive approach to non-sexual dual relationships, whilst maintaining the unacceptability of exploiting clients or having a sexual relationship with them. In their *Code of Conduct, Ethical Principles and Guidelines* (1998) there is a section on personal conduct in which it states that psychologists 'shall not exploit any relationship of influence or trust which exists between colleagues, those under their tuition, or those in receipt of their services to further the gratification of their personal wishes'. This is supplemented for counselling psychologists with 'Guidelines for the Professional Practice of Counselling Psychology', in which it states that 'therapeutic relationships expressly preclude sexual relationships and all boundary issues will be discussed with the supervisor/consultant and it is the practitioner's responsibility to define and maintain clear and appropriate boundaries'. This is compatible with the approach in the codes of ethics and practice of BAC(P) published between 1984 and 1998.

Between 1998 and 2001 there was a radical rethink by members of BACP who had been involved in the development of these codes. Over the 14 years the codes had got considerably longer, as was mentioned earlier, and the language, and therefore the tenor, of the codes had changed. In the first code published in 1984 the common phrases are that counsellors 'have a responsibility to', or 'are responsible for'; and the injunctions are verbs like 'monitor', 'respect', 'take account of'. In later codes there are many more imperatives, with 'must' being used very frequently, and less space for counsellors to take responsibility for their decisions. Pattison (1999) pointed out that one unintended consequence of all these strictures was that they did 'little to develop or support the active independent critical judgement and discernment that should be associated with true moral responsibility'; and they did not 'foster and elicit ethical awareness or behaviour'. Another concern was that the approach that had been adopted was to alter the codes every time a new professional issue arose. With the proliferation of counselling, practitioners were working in new settings, each one of which brought new professional challenges and therefore needed a new code of practice. There was a danger of an endless proliferation of new codes and the rewriting of the old ones. A small committee led by Tim Bond tackled the problem of whether there was another approach to ethical practice that would involve the practitioners in thinking about and then making ethical decisions, for which they could take responsibility which they could and justify to their colleagues if necessary. Professional ethicists were consulted and the outcome was an *Ethical Framework for Good Practice in Counselling and Psychotherapy* published for consultation in 2001 and adopted by the Association, after some alterations, in 2002. This document outlines the core values and ethical principles of counselling and the personal moral qualities to which practitioners should aspire. These are then backed up by 'Guidance on Good Practice in Counselling and Psychotherapy', which takes into account the diversity of settings in which therapists work and is not so rooted in Western ways of thinking. These supersede all the previously published codes of ethics and practice, and 'practitioner' is used throughout to mean a therapist working in any sphere, whether 'counsellor, psychotherapist, trainer, educator, supervisor, researcher, provider of counselling skills or manager of any of these services'. From the point of view of boundaries, overlapping relationships and role conflict there are three relevant clauses:

- Dual relationships arise when the practitioner has two or more kinds of relationship concurrently with a client, for example client and trainee, acquaintance and client, colleague and supervisee. The existence of a dual relationship with a client is seldom neutral and can have a powerful beneficial or detrimental impact that may not always be easily foreseeable. For these reasons practitioners are required to consider the implications of entering into dual relationships with clients, to avoid entering into relationships that are likely to be detrimental to clients, and to be readily accountable to clients and colleagues for any dual relationships that occur. (4)
- Practitioners must not abuse their client's trust in order to gain sexual, emotional, financial or any other kind of personal advantage. Sexual relations with clients are prohibited. 'Sexual relations' include intercourse, any other type of sexual activity or sexualised behaviour. Practitioners should think carefully about, and exercise considerable caution before, entering into personal or business relationships with former clients and should expect to be professionally accountable if the relationship becomes detrimental to the client or the standing of the profession. (18)

- Conflicts of interest are best avoided, provided they can be reasonably foreseen in the first instance and prevented from arising. In deciding how to respond to conflicts of interest, the protection of the client's interests and maintaining trust in the practitioner should be paramount. (55)

All the issues raised in this book are those of those of practitioners trying to work ethically in very varying circumstances. The conclusions I have reached have arisen from my own experience and that of others who have wrestled with these problems. The clauses mentioned above are consistent with the conclusions reached by people who have found themselves to be boundary riders practising on the edge and trying to evolve practice that met clients' needs, however unusual they were.

There are two remaining questions from the first chapter of this book. Why are the professional associations of therapists much more circumspect about non-sexual dual relationships than other professions? Are therapists right to be wary, and if so, are they in the vanguard, setting an example that these other professions should follow? I believe that therapists, because part of their job is to listen to the abused and damaged people in our society, are inevitably aware of the damage that people suffer when professionals cross boundaries. This will make them hyper-alert to the abuse of power which can so often happen when dual relationships are formed. For this reason alone therapists will take care about boundaries and veer to the cautious side. In addition part of the ethos of therapists in Western cultures has been to foster the autonomy of the individual: thus one of the therapeutic tasks has been to help break the silence of the abused minority and diminish secrecy, fostering transparency. This has meant that, although the system is far from perfect, complaints are encouraged and taken seriously. The result has been that trainees are able to complain about the effect of non-sexual dual relationships on courses and as a consequence the first *Code of Ethics and Practice for Trainers* (BAC, 1985) addressed this problem. All this means that the very nature of the job involves therapists in being aware of the existence of abusive non-sexual dual relationships and therefore having something to tell other professions. However, sometimes the fear of damaging clients has meant that some of the rules have become too rigid and resulted in a prescriptive approach to ethical practice rather than a one in which professional accountability is paramount. In this respect the approach of other professions in which practitioners are expected to act with probity, according to long-established but largely unwritten rules, and to be accountable to their peers for their behaviour is desirable, and BACP has achieved this after a mere 25 years. The other professions do need to listen to the experience of therapists, which is that they should take much more care with non-sexual dual relationships, because they can be damaging and the imbalance of power can lead to people being reluctant or unable to complain.

My last task is to look to the future. Other cultures are challenging therapists to think even more broadly about their ways of working. In other words, there are still unexplored edges for the boundary riders.

Future

Gabriel (2001) in her recent research has found ample evidence that non-sexual dual relationships can be as abusive as sexual ones, with the emotional and psychological impact mirroring that of a sexual dual relationship. She interviewed people who found that the 'relational benefits counterbalanced the role conflicts and challenges'. Significantly Gabriel discovered marked differences in the characteristics of those who benefited from the experience and those who did not. Broadly these were that those who were debilitated or damaged were less robust, having 'difficulties in sustaining self in various relationship roles', appearing 'unable to say "no" to the therapist' and being unable to 'assert their rights, concerns or problems'; whereas those who gained were 'sufficiently personally empowered to be able to fully enter into and intervene and challenge in either the therapy relationship or the overlapping roles'.

It is clear from this research that managing multiple roles is not for the inexperienced therapist and even with experience there should be training as well. The training should cover areas such as assessment, so that therapists recognise that if a dual relationship is unavoidable then those who are less robust are handled with extreme care; supervision must be regular and the client should be consulted right from the outset. In consulting with the client, the therapist must be aware that one of the hardest things for the less robust clients is to say what they feel and mean, and they will, therefore, appear to acquiesce to a dual relationship. Training must also focus on the complexity of managing these relationships and encourage the therapists to be reflective and not to act on impulse: reflective means expecting unexpected happenings.

The future is not simply about learning from research undertaken in the UK, albeit extremely important research. It is also about recognising the global culture and multiculturalism in all parts of the world. Counselling and psychotherapy have grown up in the Western world, so many practices need to be looked at from other perspectives. Lago and Thompson (1996) argue that Western forms of knowledge tend to be external, based on measuring and quantifying, with the seeker after knowledge trying to be objective and distanced from the object. In both Western European and the North American cultures individual self-worth has been the primary goal (Waldegrave, 1990); whereas Asian (Sue and Sue, 1990), Indian, African (Lartey, 1999), Maori and Pacific Island people (Waldegrave, 1990) come from communal and extended family cultures where internal and external ways of knowing are valued, and the cohesiveness of the family group and integration of mind, body and spirit is the goal. In these cultures questions about the self are alienating and insensitive when the framework of meaning comes from a family consensus. In the case of Maori and Samoan people, for instance, when an issue is particularly sensitive, such as sexual abuse, one person is given spokesperson's rights for the family. Attempts to bring other members of a family, including the abuser, into the discussion would be resisted and treated with embarrassment.

There are many examples of working therapeutically with the whole family from around the world. All these challenge the Western focus on the individual. At an International Association for Counselling conference held in India in 2001 the Indian therapists and social workers spoke of the importance of the family and how the whole family, and even the village community, has to be used to help someone with a problem such as alcoholism. This they described as the 'third force'. If the whole community were not involved then the person would not recover.

Another example is a group in New Zealand called 'Just Therapy'. Their aim is to give culturally appropriate therapy for Maori and Pacific Island people. Part of this approach is to reject simply working intrapsychically and to work in a broader context. This leads 'to eat[ing] communally, mak[ing] decisions consensually, receiv[ing] and farewell[ing] [sic] guests formally and traditionally, and shar[ing] and express[ing] different forms of spirituality'; but it also means that the therapists are informed about the 'gender, cultural, social and economic context of those seeking help' and make sure that these are talked about in the therapeutic sessions (Waldegrave, 1990). Thus if someone is depressed because of unemployment, they are helped to identify which problems are not of their own making, but a consequence of political and economic decisions made by local or central government. The therapists are employed in local community development projects, where they frequently work with their clients who are encouraged to promote justice. Hence forming dual relationships is the norm for these therapists originally trained in New Zealand in the Western tradition.

In every society there are people on low income, in substandard housing, attending under-resourced schools with lower standards of education. Generally therapy is not available to them but is available to the middle classes. It is not only that therapy is not available but the practical issues like illiteracy, hunger and unemployment are either more important than any emotional problems or contribute to them. This has resulted in a movement in the US towards social advocacy, which means an approach to working with clients similar to that of the Just Therapy group in New Zealand. I have more than once worked in the UK with clients with multiple problems, where simply being their counsellor seemed to be almost perverse and certainly unhelpful. Issues such as the inability to fill in a form because they were barely literate, or not knowing how to get a child into nursery, or such little knowledge of parent-craft that the children were suffering, were as important as the deprivation of warm and loving relationships as a child. In this type of situation keeping trust might mean working in a variety of roles that are sensitive to the cultural, economic and social situation of the client. Psychotherapists working in the UK for the Medical Foundation with victims of torture also find that they have to work in unconventional ways. Their clients have survived torture and lived in countries where agents of the state often violate fundamental human rights. Unsurprisingly, when they arrive in the UK seeking asylum they have multiple problems, such as housing, language and financial difficulties, quite apart from the trauma from the torture and the loss of the ability to trust anyone. All these issues need attention before actual psychotherapy can start. Once it does start, trust will be a major therapeutic issue. This means that to gain trust the therapists have to have multiple roles and to do such things as invite other family members to sessions.

Perhaps the challenge for the next generation of boundary riders is how to manage these very complex relationships with a different set of multiple roles. They will have to find ways to do this that do not exploit or abuse the clients but are life enhancing. It can be seen from this book that exploring and defining the limits is a very complex task and demands sensitivity, a capacity to imagine the unimaginable and the courage to be a boundary rider on the edge of experience.

Appendix: Useful Addresses

British Association for Counselling and Psychotherapy (BACP)
1 Regent Place
Rugby
CV21 2PJ
Telephone number: 0870 4435252
Website: *www.bacp.co.uk*

British Confederation of Psychotherapists (BCP)
37 Mapesbury Road
London
NW2 4HJ
Telephone number: 020 8830 5173
Website: *www.bcp.org.uk*

British Psychological Society (BPS)
St Andrew's House
48 Princess Road East
Leicester
LE1 7DR
Telephone number: 0116 254 9568
Website: *www.bps.org.uk*

Prevention of Professional Abuse Network (POPAN)
1 Wyvil Court
Wyvil Road
London
SW8 2TG
Telephone number: 020 7622 6334
Website: *www.popan.org.uk*

United Kingdom Council for Psychotherapy (UKCP)
167–169 Great Portland Street
London
W1N 5FB
Telephone number: 020 7436 3002
Website: *www.psychotherapy.org.uk*

Bibliography

American Counseling Association (1997), *Code of Ethics and Standards of Practice*, Alexandria, MD: American Counseling Association.

Amos, T. and Margison, F. (1998), 'Gifts in Psychotherapy', Abstract in *Proceedings of Society for Psychotherapy Research International Conference*, Snowbird, Utah, USA, 24–28 June.

Association of Occupational Therapists (2000), *Code of Ethics and Professional Conduct for Occupational Therapists*, London: College of Occupational Therapists.

Bond, Tim (2000), *Standards and Ethics for Counselling in Action*, 2nd edn. London: Sage (1st edn, 1993).

British Association for Counselling (BAC) (1984), *Code of Ethics and Practice for Counsellors*, Rugby: British Association for Counselling.

British Association for Counselling (BAC) (1985), *Code of Ethics and Practice for Trainers*, Rugby: British Association for Counselling.

British Association for Counselling (BAC) (1988), *Code of Ethics and Practice for the Supervision of Counsellors*, Rugby: British Association for Counselling.

British Association for Counselling (BAC) (1990), *Code of Ethics and Practice for Counsellors*, Rugby: British Association for Counselling.

British Association for Counselling (BAC) (1993), *Code of Ethics and Practice for Counsellors*, Rugby: British Association for Counselling.

British Association for Counselling (BAC) (1995), *Code of Ethics and Practice for Trainers*, Rugby: British Association for Counselling.

British Association for Counselling (BAC) (1996a), *Code of Ethics and Practice for Supervisors*, Rugby: British Association for Counselling.

British Association for Counselling (BAC) (1996b), *Ethical Guidelines for Monitoring, Evaluation and Research in Counselling*, Rugby: British Association for Counselling.

British Association for Counselling (BAC) (1998), *Code of Ethics and Practice for Counsellors*, Rugby: British Association for Counselling.

British Association for Counselling and Psychotherapy (BACP) (2002), *Ethical Framework for Good Practice in Counselling and Psychotherapy*, Rugby: British Association for Counselling and Psychotherapy.

British Psychological Society (BPS) (1998), *Code of Conduct, Ethical Principles and Guidelines*, Leicester: British Psychological Society.

Clarkson, P. (1995), *The Therapeutic Relationship*, London: Whurr.

Cooper, J. (1993), *Speak of Me As I Am: the Life and Work of Masud Khan*, London: Karnac Books.

Dinnage, R. (1989), *One to One. Experiences of Psychotherapy*, Harmondsworth: Penguin.

Diocese of Oxford (1996), *Code of Ministerial Practice*, Oxford: Oxford Diocese Office of Communications.

Disch, E. (1992), *Are You in Trouble with a Client?* Boston: BASTA! Boston Associates to Stop Treatment Abuse.

Douthwaite, R. (1996), 'Reclaiming Community: Steps to Building a Healthy Local Economy', *New Internationalist*, April: 26–27.

France, A. (1988), *Consuming Psychotherapy*, London: Free Association Books.

Freud, S. (1915), 'Observations on Transference Love', in Standard Edition, Volume XII. Trans. James Strachey. London: Hogarth.

Freud, S. and Breuer, J. (1895), *Studies on Hysteria*, Penguin Freud Library, Volume III, Harmondsworth: Penguin.

Gabbard, G.O. (1995), 'Countertransference: The Emerging Common Ground', *International Journal of Psycho-Analysis*, 76: 475–485.

Gabriel, L. (2000), 'Dual Relationships in Organisational Contexts', *Counselling*, 11: 17–19.

Gabriel, L. (2001), 'Speaking the Unspeakable: Dual Relationships in Counselling and Psychotherapy,' Unpublished doctoral thesis, York St John (A College of the University of Leeds).

Gabriel, L. and Davies, D. (2000), 'The Management of Ethical Dilemmas Associated with Dual Relationships', in Neal, C. and Davies, D. (eds), *Issues in Therapy with Lesbian, Gay, Bisexual and Transgender Clients*, Buckingham: Open University Press.

Garrett, T. (1994), 'Sexual Contact between Psychotherapists and their Patients', in Clarkson, P. and Pokorny, M. (eds), *The Handbook of Psychotherapy*, London: Routledge.

Gerrard, J. (1996), 'Love in the Time of Psychotherapy', *British Journal of Psychotherapy*, 13: 163–173.

Gray, A. (1994), *An Introduction to the Therapeutic Frame*, London: Routledge.

Greenberg, J. and Mitchell, S.A. (1983), *Object Relations in Psychoanalytic Practice*, Cambridge, MA: Harvard University Press.

Greenspan, M. (1994), 'On Professionalism', in Heyward, C. (ed.), *When Boundaries Betray Us*, New York: HarperSanFrancisco.

Guthmann, D. and Sandberg, K.A. (2002), 'Dual Relationships in the Deaf Community: When Dual Relationships are Unavoidable and Essential', in Lazarus, A.A. and Zur, O. (eds), *Dual Relationships and Psychotherapy*, New York: Springer.

Heimann, P. (1950), 'On Counter-Transference', *International Journal of Psychoanalysis*, 31: 81–84.

Hetherington, A. (2000), 'A Psychodynamic Profile of Therapists who Sexually Exploit their Clients', *British Journal of Psychotherapy*, 16: 274–286.

Heyward, C. (1994), *When Boundaries Betray Us*, New York: HarperSanFrancisco.

Hinshelwood, R.D. (1999), 'Countertransference', *International Journal of Psychoanalysis*, 80: 797–818.

Hirsch, I. and Kessel, P. (1988), 'Reflections on Mature Love and Countertransference', *Free Associations*, 12: 60–83.

Howard, E.J. (2002), *Slipstream, A Memoir*, Basingstoke: Macmillan.

Hunter, M. and Struve, J. (1998), *The Ethical Use of Touch in Psychotherapy*, Thousand Oaks, CA: Sage.

Jacobs, M. (1992), *Sigmund Freud*, London: Sage.

Jacobs, M. (1995), *D.W. Winnicott*, London: Sage.

Jacobs, T.J. (1999), 'Countertransference Past and Present: a Review of the Concept', *International Journal of Psychoanalysis*, 80: 575–594.

Kahn, M.M.R. (1988), *When Spring Comes*, London: Chatto & Windus.

Kahr, B. (1996), *D.W. Winnicott: A Biographical Portrait*, London: Karnac Books.

Lago, C. and Thompson, J. (1996), *Race, Culture and Counselling*, Buckingham: Open University Press.

Lartey, E. (1999), 'Pastoral Counselling in Multi-cultural Contexts', in Lynch, G. (ed.), *Clinical Counselling in Pastoral Settings*, London: Routledge.

Lazarus, A.A. and Zur, O. (2002), 'Introduction', in Lazarus, A.A. and Zur, O. (eds), *Dual Relationships and Psychotherapy*, New York: Springer.

Little, M. (1985), 'Winnicott Working in Areas where Psychotic Anxieties Predominate: a Personal Record', *Free Associations*, 3: 9–42.

Lomas, P. (1987), *The Limitations of Interpretation*, Harmondsworth: Penguin.

Longman (1991), *Dictionary of the English Language*, Harlow: Longman.

Lott, D.A. (1999), 'Drawing Boundaries. (Recognising Structure and Boundaries in Patient–Therapist Interactions)' *Psychology Today* (*http://www.findarticles.com/cf_1/m1175/3_32/54504419/print.jhtml*)

Lyall, M. (1997), *The Pastoral Counselling Relationship. A Touching Place?* Contact Pastoral Monograph Number 7. Edinburgh: Contact Pastoral Trust.

Lynch, G. (1999), 'Dual Relationships in Pastoral Counselling', in Lynch, G. (ed.), *Clinical Counselling in Pastoral Settings*, London: Routledge.

Lynch, G. (2002), *Pastoral Care and Counselling*, London: Sage.

Mann, D. (1997), *Psychotherapy: an Erotic Relationship*, London: Routledge.

Mann, D. (ed.) (1999), *Erotic Transference and Countertransference*, London: Routledge.

Maslow, A. (1962), *Toward a Psychology of Being*, Princeton, NJ: Van Nostrand.

McLeod, J. (1999), *Practitioner Research in Counselling*, London: Sage.

Milner, M. (1969), *In the Hands of the Living God: a Personal Account of a Psycho-Analytic Treatment*, London: Hogarth Press.

Mitchell, S.A. (1993), *Hope and Dread in Psychoanalysis*, New York: Basic Books.

Orbach, S. (1999), *The Impossibility of Sex*, Harmondsworth: Allen Lane.

Parkes, C.M. (2001), quoted by Julia Stuart in *The Independent*, 31 October.

Pattison, S. (1999), 'Are Professional Codes Ethical?', *Counselling*, 10: 374–380.

Paul, S. and Pelham, G. (2000), 'A Relational Approach to Therapy', in Palmer, S. and Woolfe, R. (eds), *An Integrative Approach to Therapy*, London: Sage.

Pope, K.S., Sonne, J.L. and Holroyd, J. (1993), *Sexual Feelings in Psychotherapy: Explanations for Therapists and Therapists-in-Training*, Washington, DC: American Psychological Association.

Prodgers, A. (1996), 'Touch and Psychotherapy', *Changes*, 4: 189–192.

Rayner, E. (1993), 'Foreword', in Cooper, J., *Speak of Me As I Am: The Life and Work of Masud Khan*, London: Karnac Books.

Rosenberg, V. (1995), 'On Touching a Patient', *British Journal of Psychotherapy*, 12: 29–36.

Ross, A. (1999), 'The Place of Religious Tradition in Pastoral Counselling', in Lynch, G. (ed.), *Clinical Counselling in Pastoral Settings*, London: Routledge.

Russell, J. (1993), *Out of Bounds. Sexual Exploitation in Counselling and Therapy*, London: Sage.

Rutter, P. (1990), *Sex in the Forbidden Zone*, London: Unwin Paperbacks.

Sands, A. (2000), *Falling for Therapy*, Basingstoke: Macmillan.

Schaverien, J. (1997), 'Men Who Leave Too Soon: Reflections on the Erotic Transference and Countertransference', *British Journal of Psychotherapy*, 14: 3–16.

Smith, E.W.L. (1998a), 'A Taxonomy and Ethics of Touch in Psychotherapy', in Smith, E.W.L., Clance, P.R. and Imes, S. (eds), *Touch in Psychotherapy Theory, Research and Practice*, New York: The Guildford Press. Chapter 3.

Smith, E.W.L. (1998b), 'Tradition of Touch in Psychotherapy', in Smith, E.W.L., Clance, P.R. and Imes, S. (eds), *Touch in Psychotherapy Theory, Research and Practice*, New York: The Guildford Press. Chapter 1.

Smith, E.W.L., Clance, P.R. and Imes, S. (eds) (1998), *Touch in Psychotherapy. Theory, Research, and Practice*, New York: The Guildford Press.

Spandler, H., Burman, E., Goldberg, B., Margison, F. and Amos, T. (2000), '"A Double-Edged Sword": Understanding Gifts in Psychotherapy', *European Journal of Psychotherapy, Counselling and Health*, 3: 77–101.

Stern, S. (1994), 'Needed Relationships and Repeated Relationships: an Integrated Relational Perspective', *Psychoanalytic Dialogues*, 4: 317–345.

Sue, D.W. and Sue, D. (1990), *Counselling the Culturally Different*, New York: Wiley.

Sue, S. and Zane, N. (1987), 'The Role of Culture and Cultural Techniques in Psychotherapy: a Critique and Reformulation', *American Psychologist*, 42: 37–45.

Syme, G. (1994), *Counselling in Independent Practice*, Buckingham: Open University Press.

Tune, D. (2001), 'Is Touch a Valid Therapeutic Intervention? Early Returns from a Quantitative Study of Therapists' Views', *Counselling and Psychotherapy Research*, 1: 167–171.

United Kingdom Council for Psychotherapy (UKCP) (1998), *Ethical Requirements of Member Organisations*, London: United Kingdom Council for Psychotherapy.

Waldegrave, C. (1990), 'Just Therapy', *Dulwich Centre Newsletter*, 1: 3–47.

Wehr, G. (1985), *Jung: a Biography*, Boston: Shambhala.

Welles, J.K. and Wrye, H.K. (1991), 'The Maternal Erotic Countertransference', *International Journal of Psycho-Analysis*, 72: 93–106.

Wheeler, S. (1996), ' Facing Death with a Client: Confrontation or Collusion, Counter Transference or Compassion?', *Psychodynamic Counselling*, 2: 167–178.

Woodmansey, A.C. (1988), 'Are Psychotherapists Out of Touch?', *British Journal of Psychotherapy*, 5: 57–65.

Index